C000265114

The Unbelief of St. Thomas the Apostle, Laid Open, for the Comfort of All That Desire to Believe. Repr

THE

UNBELIEF

OF

ST. THOMAS THE APOSTLE,

LAID OPEN

FOR THE COMFORT OF ALL THAT DESIRE

TO BELIEVE;

which armeth us against despair
in the hour of death.

By NICHOLAS BOWNDE,

DOCTOR IN DIVINITY.

FIRST PRINTED IN 1608.

LONDON:

REPRINTED BY AND FOR NICHOLS, SON, & BENTLEY,
RED LION PASSAGE, FLEET STREET. SOLD ALSO
BY T. COMBE, LEICESTER; AND J. BOTTRILL, LUT-
TERWORTH.

1817.

100. S. 429.

THE
UNBELIEF
OF
ST. THOMAS THE APOSTLE.

John c. 20, v. 24, &c.

But Thomas, one of the twelve, called Didymus, was
not with them when Jesus came. 25. The other
Disciples therefore said unto him, We have seen the
Lord: but he said unto them, Except I see in his
hands the print of the nails, and put my finger
into the print of the nails, and put mine hand into
his side, I will not believe it. 26. And eight days
after again his disciples were within, and Thomas
with them. Then came Jesus, when the doors were
shut, and stood in the midst, and said, Peace be
unto you. 27. After, he said to Thomas, Put thy
finger here, and see mine hands, and put forth
thine hand, and put it into my side: and be not
faithless, but faithful. 28. Then Thomas answered,
and said unto him, My Lord, and my God. 29.
Jesus said unto him, Thomas, because thou hast
seen me, thou believest: blessed are they, that have
not seen, and have believed.

THIS text of Scripture is appointed to be
read for the Gospel upon St. Thomas's
Day, because it containeth a memorable
story of him, whose blessed memory we
keep upon that day: to that end, that we

might be thankful unto God for him, and for the excellent gifts bestowed upon him, and the great good done to the Church by his ministry and preaching: and that we might labour to imitate his virtues, and to profit by his great infirmities: wherein consisteth the true and right observation of this, and all other such like days.

And not in the worshipping of him, and praying to him, and setting up candles before his image, and offering to him, as they did in the time of Popery; when they prayed unto God to be heard at his intercession, and for his merits, and blood shedding; as they did upon other such days for the rest of the Apostles and Saints. And they thought that the celebrating of those days was a great honour and service acceptable unto them, and they kept them to that end, that they might become their patrons, and fare the better for their sakes before God: and they know no other use of them unto this day.

Wherein they offer great indignity unto Christ, first, in robbing and spoiling him of the honour and office of his mediation and intercession, to whom only it belongeth: of whom the Apostle thus writeth :— it is Christ which is dead, yea or rather

which is risen again (Rom. c. 8, v. 24):
who is also at the right hand of God, and
maketh request also for us, and therefore
who shall lay any thing to the charge of
God's chosen? And Christ himself thus
speaketh of his own office (John c. 14,
v. 13): Whatsoever ye ask in my name,
that will I do, that the Father may be glorified in the Son.

Secondly, they do great wrong unto him,
in hallowing any days to the honour of
any, but of God alone. For all things that
are sanctified, are sanctified to his honour
and worship only, who only is to be wor-
shipped and served with divine worship:
therefore the bread and wine in the sacra-
ment of the Lord's supper, and the water
in baptism, are sanctified to the honour of
Christ, and of none other: as those that
represent unto us the breaking of his body,
and the shedding of his most precious
blood for the forgiveness of our sins. And
so are and ought the Churches to be con--
secrated to the name and honour of God
alone (who only is there to be served), and
not of any Saint, as in time past they have
been.

And so ought the days also: as under
the law all the Sabbaths were consecrated.

unto the honour of God, the creator of heaven and earth: and under the Gospel unto the honour of Christ the Redeemer of his Church: and all other days, that are now put apart among us from the common affairs of the world, they are sanctified to that end, that God might be honoured in them, and by them.

And therefore we put a great difference between these holy days, and the Sabbath, or Lord's day. First of all in that we know this latter to stand upon a better foundation than they, as having his institution from Christ and his Apostles, and so doth bind all nations, and is perpetual; never to be changed. Whereas the former have their warrant only from men, and so do not bind all Churches alike, and may be changed, yea taken clean away: and serve only for Christian policy, and good order in the Church, that men upon these days might come together, and serve God. And therefore it is to be provided, that there should not be too many of them, lest thereby men should be hindered from the necessary works of their callings; which hath moved the Reformed Churches, as in this realm, so elsewhere, to cut off many that were used in the time of Popery, and so to keep themselves in a mediocrity, neither having too many, nor putting down all.

Secondly, there is a difference between them, in the manner of keeping the one, and the other: for on the Christian Sabbath the laws of our kingdom and Church do restrain all men from many things, as from markets, and fairs, and keeping of assizes and sessions for the execution of justice: which they do tolerate and permit upon other holydays. Whereas in the time of blindness they sometimes preferred these days before the Sabbath; and had more so- lemn service and feasts upon them, and counted it a more deadly sin then to work, than upon the Sabbath-day.

Besides this, they appointing these days to the honour of men, did thereby greatly dishonour the Saints themselves. For what greater dishonour can there be unto any man, than to make him a traitor? and to give unto him that honour, that is due only to the Prince? And if any should in simplicity and good-will ascribe so much to the great- est nobleman in the realm, that at the last he should give him the titles that belong unto the King, and so bring him into the suspicion of treason against his will, it were no honour, but dishonour unto him : so the Papists in extolling the Saints so highly, that they consecrate days unto them, and thereby seek to honour them, and hope that therefore they will become patrons unto them : all which are proper unto Christ; in so doing they dishonour them : for they make them, as much as lieth in them, to be traitors unto Christ, in robbing him of that honour that is proper unto him. The Angel would not suffer St. John to worship him (Rev. c. 22, v. 8 and 9).

And these Saints, if they were now alive upon earth, would not only not take this honour unto themselves, and thank them for it, but altogether refuse it, and rebuke them for it; as Paul and Barnabas did unto the people at Lystra, when they brought bulls with garlands, and would have sacrificed unto them : they rent their cloathes, and ran in among them (Acts c. 14, v. 14), saying, O men, why do you these things ? we are men subject unto the like passions, that you be : and preach unto you, that you should turn from these vain things unto the living God.

In this text there are these four things principally to be observed : first of all the great infidelity of St. Thomas the Apostle, who did not believe the resurrection of Christ, reported unto him by all his fellow Apostles, who had seen him (v. 24, 25). Secondly, the great mercy of Christ, who did not cast him off, and leave him to perish in this unbelief of his, but most lovingly in time convenient sought to pull him out of it by all good means ; even the very same, which himself desired (ver. 26, 27). Thirdly, the increase of faith in Thomas by these means, appearing by the confession that he made, after that he was thus confirmed, namely, that he did believe, not only that he was risen again, but for him, and therefore calleth him, his Lord and his God (ver. 28). Lastly, here Christ upon this occasion delivereth a general doctrine, and so applieth this fact of Thomas unto the whole Church ; even that they should be blessed who should believe in him, though they did not see him, as he had done.

I do not purpose to intreat of all these, but only of so much, as doth concern the unbelief of St. Thomas. But before I come

to it, it may seem somewhat strange, that
St. John in his Gospel doth write this of
his fellow Apostle, seeing it tendeth so
wholly to his discredit. The other Evangelists all of them have left it out, it may
seem in favour of him; and it might be
thought, that it had been better, if he had
passed it over with silence also. But this
Apostle living longer than all the rest,
about an hundred years after Christ, and
so seeing all their writings, doth add this,
as a matter of special moment: as indeed
in it there is offered to the Church great
instruction and consolation.

And this plain dealing of his is a note of
that integrity, that is to be found in all the
Scriptures, as being penned by the Spirit
of God. For they came not in old time,
as St. Peter saith (2 Peter, c. 1, v. 21), by
the will of man: but holy men of God did
speak and write as they were moved by
the Holy Ghost. And therefore they
greatly differ from the writings of men,
which savour of the spirit of men; and so
are in many things partial: as this is a
common fault in many historiographers,
that they flatter great men, and speak only
of their virtues, which they set out to the
full; but their vices either they wholly

conceal, or lightly pass them over; especially when they are their friends, and of the same rank and order with them, as St. Thomas was unto the Apostle St. John. But it is not so in the Scriptures, which proceeding from the Spirit of Truth, are no more partial than God himself, with whom there is no respect of persons (Rom. c. 2, v. 11): insomuch that the penners of them do lay open the greatest sins of the greatest men in their time, even of the Kings and of the Priests.

As of Heli, how he honoured his children above God, and caused the sacrifices of the Lord to be despised, and trodden under foot (1 Sam. c. 2, v. 28): and of Manasseh king of Judah, how he caused his sons to pass through the fire in the valley of Ben-hinnom, and gave himself to witchcraft, and to charming, and to sorcery: and used them that had familiar spirits, and soothsayers: and did very much evil in the sight of the Lord, to anger him (2 Chr. c. 3, v. 6): yea, the Prophets do not spare them that were nearest in blood to them, or nearest in any bond of affinity, or friendship. For Moses doth set out the murmuring of Aaron, his own natural brother, and of his sister

Miriam, and how God did punish them for it (Num. c. 12, v. 2) : which he did not to defame them, or with a mind to be revenged of them : for the Lord gave this testimony of him, that he was a very meek man, above all the men that were upon the earth (ver. 3).

And the Apostles do write the truth boldly and sincerely of their fellow Apostles, though their faults were exceeding great, and not the like almost heard of. As how Judas did for thirty pieces of silver sell and betray his Lord and Master Christ into the hands of his most deadly enemies (Matt. c. 26, v. 15). And how Peter did not only deny him once, but the second time did forswear him (ver. 70), yea did curse and bann himself, if that ever he did but know him.

And to conclude this point, their uprightness in their writings appeareth so much the more, that they do not spare themselves, but publish their own faults to the praise of God, as his spirit in them did direct them. For Moses declareth at large how slow and backward he was to take upon him that calling, that God had appointed him unto, and what excuses and delays he made, insomuch that the Lord was very angry with him (Exod. c. 4, v. 14).

And David writeth of the adultery and murder, that he had secretly committed against Bathsheba, and her husband Uriah: and confesseth openly, that he had deserved death for both of them, when he thus prayeth (Psal. 51, v. 14), Deliver me from blood, O Lord. So likewise the Apostle Paul spareth not himself, because it was not he, but the Spirit of God that spake in him, in that he had persecuted the Church of God cruelly, and wasted it (Gal. c. 1, v. 13). This kind of simple dealing is one argument not of the least moment, among many other, to evince that the Scriptures are written by God's Spirit: and are therefore Canonical, for they are not partial: but the spirit of truth and simple dealing doth marvellously appear every where in them.

But it may further be demanded, though such things as these be written of the Saints, whether they should be read openly in the Church upon those holy days, that carry their name: as if, when we keep the memory of a man, all his evil deeds should be reckoned up, tending to his infamy and discredit. Concerning which, as the

Providence of God therein is to be acknow-
ledged, who hath thus disposed of it, so
we are to reverence and highly esteem the
godly wisdom of those holy fathers, who
did first appoint those days thus to be kept.
For they did it to the honour of God, and
therefore would by the reading of these
texts of Scripture have all men know, what
the Saints were of themselves : and what
infirmities, unbelief, and other sins they
were subject unto; even the same that we
are: as Paul and Barnabas said of themselves (Acts c. 14, v. 14), We are men, subject to the like passions that you are: and
as St. James saith of the Prophet Elias
(Jam. c. 5, v. 17), that he was a man subject to the like passions as we are. That so
if they were any thing, we might know
from whence it came, and so as Paul saith
of himself (1 Cor. c. 15, v. 9), I am the
least of the Apostles, which am not worthy
to be called an Apostle, because I persecuted the Church of God : but by the grace
of God, I am that I am : and his grace
which is in me, was not in vain : but I la-
boured more abundantly than they all ;
yet not I, but the grace of God which is
with me. So we might say of them, being
put in mind by the Scriptures that are read

even upon those days, wherein we keep the greatest memory of them, what they were of themselves, and what they were by the grace of God; and so not so much honour them, as praise God for them.

For the purpose of those ancient fathers of the Church, who appointed these days thus to be kept, was not to set out the Saints themselves, that we might glory in them, and in their merits; but in the merits of Christ, and in the mercy of God shewed to them for his sake: and so not only to teach us how rightly to esteem of them, but that in them, as in a glass, we might see what we are subject unto: and yet how gracious God is to poor sinners, and so might take comfort in the mercy of God shewed to them. As here what great uubelief was in St. Thomas, and yet Christ did help him of it, and saved him? to shew us, that we are as full of unbelief, as he, and much more: yet Christ will not refuse us, if we do not obstinately remain in it, but are willing to be holpen of it, and have a desire to believe, by the means that he shall bestow upon us. And this is the use that we are to make of the unbelief of St. Thomas, even then when we hear it read upon his day.

The Papists did not so : for besides that they had a great number of counterfeit Saints in their Calendar, whose names were not written in the book of life ; some of them traitors, and others as ill, or worse than they: upon their festival days, they caused to be read out of *Legenda aurea,* that is, their Legend of lies, a story of their lives, full of all virtues, and miracles that they wrought, some in their life, some after their death, whereof most were feigned, and some of them most absurd. · And thus they made them to be Gods upon the earth, not making mention of any fault of their's at any time, especially so great as these that we have heard of in St. Thomas, St. Paul, and the rest.

Whereby it came to pass, partly by the observation of those days, and partly by hearing what was then reported of them out of their stories, that the common people were brought into a superstitious admiration of them, and had no hope by imitating their virtues to be like them : but rather did worship them by means of the strange and incredible things that they heard of them. And so there was no comfort from them for poor sinners, but only for their merits and mediation : for they did not speak of their infirmities and falls. But we see, how the Scriptures set out the true Saints of God after another manner; not only in their miracles and virtues, but in their greatest corruptions and sins; that we knowing what they were of themselves, and what they are by the mercy of God, and the grace of Christ, the poorest sinners might be comforted in themselves by the one, and give thanks to God for the other. Seeing that there is no sin in themselves, which they have not seen pardoned and cured in some of the Saints or other: nor any grace wanting to themselves, which by that experience of God's goodness which they have seen in others, they might not hope for in themselves in some measure.

But I come to the principal thing in this text, which is the great infirmity and wonderful unbelief that was in the Apostle St. Thomas, declared in these words of his own, that when the rest of the Disciples had told him, that they had seen the Lord, he answered them, Except I see in his hands the print of the nails, and put my finger into the print of the nails, and put mine hand into his side, I will not believe it.

The circumstance of time, and many occurrences going before this, do aggravate the greatness of his unbelief. For this was done the eighth day after Christ's resurrection: then he did shew himself unto Thomas, as it is said, (ver. 26) Eight days after his Disciples were again within, and Thomas with them, then came Jesus, when the doors were shut, and stood in the midst, and said, Peace be unto you: after he said to Thomas, Put thy finger here, and see mine hands: and put forth thine hand, and put it into my side, and be not faithless, but faithful. In the mean season he had appeared unto Mary Magdalen at the sepulchre the first day of his resurrection early in the morning, and she knew him: for he called her Mary, and she answered, Rabboni, that is to say, Master (ver. 17), at what time she was willed to go tell the Disciples, that he was risen: and she did so: and also shewed them, what other words he had spoken unto her: but none of them did believe her: as St. Mark saith (Mark c. 16, v. 11). Thus at the first hearing of it, Thomas was incredulous, as well as the rest. And the same day toward the evening, he appeared unto two other as they were in the way to Emmaus, and they

returned presently, and told the Disciples
of it, but they did not believe them neither
(ver. 13).

The same night therefore he appeared
unto the eleven, as they sate together, and
cast in their teeth their unbelief, and hardness of heart, because they believed not
them, who had now twice told them, that
they had seen him, being risen again
(ver. 14). And because their unbelief was
so great at that time, to put them out of
all doubt for the time to come, he shewed
them his hands, and his side that was
pierced, and the print of the nails in the
one, and of the spear in the other, and
bad them look on them, that they might
know that it was he indeed, as St. John the
Evangelist doth report it (John c. 20, v. 20).

At this time Thomas was not present
among them. The Lord of his infinite
wisdom and goodness thus disposing of it,
for the further good both of Thomas, and
of all the rest, and of the whole Church :
that by this means there might be a new
confirmation of his resurrection, by a second and more sensible apparition, when
they should not only see again the print of
the najls in his hands, but for Thomas also
to put his finger into them. But in the mean

while, all the rest tell him, what they had
seen, namely, not only Christ in some
form, but so certainly that he spake unto
them, and shewed them his hands and his
feet, and the print of the nails in them, so
that they could not possibly be deceived in
so clear a matter : yet for all this he not only
not giveth credit unto some one of them
severally, but not unto all of them jointly,
being so many, and so credible witnesses :
and further, is so wilful and obstinate, and
so addicted to his own senses and feeling,
that he tells them plainly, that unless he
himself see the print of the nails in his
hands, and may put his finger into them ;
and the print of the spear in his side, and
may put his hand into that, he will never
believe it.

This is a marvellous thing, and may
seem justly to be wondered at, that he
being an Apostle, and one that had been
conversant with our Saviour Christ a long
time, and had heard his doctrine, and seen
his miracles, yea, had preached salvation
in his name with the rest; and had heard
Christ often say, that he must be put to
death, and the third day rise again; that
though he did generally believe in him,
yet he was not persuaded particularly of

this article of his resurrection. But such is our corruption, and we do so receive the Spirit but in measure, that we may be true believers in general, and yet unbelievers in many particulars; as we see in the Apostle here, who believing Christ to be the son of God, and the Saviour of the world, and so held the main point of salvation, failed in the particular manner, and was not yet persuaded of the truth of his resurrection. But for all this we are not to account him, as an infidel, but think thus with ourselves, if such a man as he, was subject unto so great doubtings, no marvel then, if I in many particulars find my faith to be so full of doubting and wavering. Only let us in these doubtings still use the means, and God will at one time or other bless some of them unto us. As Thomas here not believing that Christ was risen, though the rest of the Apostles did tell him of it, did not forsake their company, but came into their assemblies upon the Lord's day to serve Christ with them, and then Christ did appear unto him, and rid him of his unbelief. Whereas if he had been still absent, as he was before, and therefore he remained longer in his unbelief than they, God might have deprived him of all means,

and justly have given him up to his unbelief.

But this is a greater wonder, and herein
his unbelief doth appear much more : that
besides the former things, when the other
Apostles, whom he by long experience
knew to be very reverend and credible men,
told him that they had seen the Lord, and
after what manner, even with the prints of
the nails, and of the spear in his body, yet
he so distrusted all of them, that he would
believe none of them. Oftentimes we believe meaner men and of less credit in matters of great uncertainty, and of small moment : therefore not to believe so many
and of so good credit, and in a thing of
great moment, it being true also, doth
plainly shew how deeply unbelief was
rooted in him. Especially if we consider
how he further addeth, that if there were
never so many more of them, let them be
what they will be, that should tell him so,
he would believe none of them, but his
own self, and his own sense and feeling :
for unless he could see in his hands the
print of the nails, and put his finger into
the print of the nails, and put his hand into
his side, he would not believe it.

And it seemeth, that the rest of the

Apostles were subject unto this unbelief, though not in the like measure: for when Mary Magdalen, at Christ's commandment, came unto them, and finding them weeping and mourning, told them for their comfort, that Christ was risen (Mark c. 16, v. 11); though they heard her say, that he was alive, and had appeared to her, they believed it not: nay they were so far from believing it, that her words seemed unto them as a feigned thing (Luke c. 24, v. 11): so that they were not only somewhat doubtful of the matter, but did wholly reject it as a mere fable. Moreover, when two of the Disciples, the name of the one being Cleopas, going to Emmaus, Christ did appear unto them in the way, and though they knew him not at the first, yet at the last their eyes were opened, so that they knew him perfectly, and so returning to Jerusalem, said unto the eleven, The Lord is risen indeed: and so do avouch it constantly with a note of asseverance; and told them also, what was done in the way, and how they knew him at the last: They believed them neither (Mark c. 16, v. 13). So that this case was not of Thomas alone, but of all the rest; that we might see that the best servants of God of all, are greatly pestered with these remnants of unbelief. That as David saith (Psal. 130, v. 3), If thou, O Lord, straightly markest iniquities, O Lord, who shall stand? that is, not the best man in the world, much less such a wretch as I. So we may say, if these holy men were so full of unbelief in this thing, no marvel, if such a poor sinner as I am, stand doubtful and perplexed in many things : and as Christ did succour them, so I hope he will be merciful unto me, that desire to believe.

And it is very probable, that the rest of the Apostles in this unbelief of their's, were subject unto the same temptations that Thomas was, and had the same thoughts to hinder them from believing that he had : and namely, that they spake within themselves as he did openly, though for shame they did not utter it, as often it falleth out, that many are afraid to utter their temptations, they are so fearful and so strange, that they think that none are possessed with them but themselves. But the Apostle telleth the Corinthians (1 Cor. c. 10, v. 13), that no temptation had taken hold of them but such as appertaineth unto man ; that is, which proceedeth of man's infirmity, and which man's nature is subject unto : that they might not be discouraged, or despair for that which he had said unto them. And therefore he addeth, that God is faithful, and would not suffer them to be tempted above that which they were able, but would give an issue with the temptation, that they might. be able to bear it : as he did here unto the rest of the Apostles, and to Thomas himself.

And that they had indeed the same thoughts of unbelief that Thomas had, appeareth by the fact of Christ. For when he came among them, and they were abashed and afraid, supposing that they had seen a spirit (Luke c. 24, v. 37), he said unto them, Why are ye troubled? and wherefore do thoughts arise in your hearts? Behold mine hands, and my feet, for it is myself; handle me, and see : and when he had thus spoken he shewed them his hands and his feet. So that Christ in shewing them his hands and feet, that so they might be rid of those thoughts and doubts that hindered them from believing, did manifestly shew, that he knew the thoughts of their hearts to be these, that unless they saw in his hands and feet the print of the nails, they would not believe that it was he. Christ therefore, like a skilful physician of their souls, did apply his medicine according to their malady; and therefore when as at his first apparition he did shew unto them his hands and his feet, he doing all things in wisdom and to some good purpose, did thereby declare, what thoughts of unbelief they were troubled with.

If such holy men as these, who had so many means to help their faith, did not sufficiently profit by them at the first; but were found thus incredulous: then we may be assured, that unbelief is more deeply rooted in us than we be aware of: and if after many means, and long continuance in the same, we find it in ourselves more than we would, we must not too much suspect ourselves, as long as we are sorry for it, and do groan under it, as under a heavy burthen, desiring to be eased of the same. For indeed, there is no sin in the world that hath more infected mankind than that: it came in with our first parents even in Paradise, and it will continue as long as there is any man upon earth: it is the first sin that possesseth all men: and it is the last that we must strive against: insomuch that when we have overcome all other, then will our unbelief most of all trouble us. And especially we shall find this to be true in all afflictions, and in the hour of death; when the temptations of pride, of voluptuousness, of revenge, &c. shall leave us, as having received their deadly blow; then will unbelief and distrust fall upon us afresh, as though it had never been wounded, or never so much as encountered with.

For seeing that faith is, as the Apostle calleth it (Eph. c. 6, v. 16), A shield wherewith we may quench all the fiery darts of the Devil: therefore he laboureth most of all to pull it out of our hands altogether, or so to weaken it in many things, that his darts may easily pierce through it into our souls to destroy them: that is, his temptation may deceive us one way or other. For as long as this shield of faith is whole, and we are able to hold it out against our spiritual enemy, we shall prevail against him, whether he tempteth us unto any sin in time to come, or for any sin of the time past. But if we let fall the shield of faith, or do not defend ourselves with it, we lie open to all temptations of Satan: that is, if we altogether give over faith, or fall to doubting of the truth of his word.

Adam and Eve were first overcome by unbelief, and that was the cause of their ruin; for the devil by disputing with the

woman like a subtle sophister, brought her
at the last to call into question the truth of
God's word, and to say, Of the fruit of the
tree, which is in the midst of the garden,
God hath said, ye shall not eat of it, neither shall ye touch it, least ye die (Gen.
c. 3, v. 3): whereas the Lord had said in
express words before (chap. 2, v. 17), In
the day that ye shall eat thereof, ye shall die
the death : that is, ye shall assuredly die :
which if they had steadfastly believed, they
had not been overcome by his temptation.
So in all sin that we commit there is unbelief, more or less; for if we fall by presumption, then we believe not his threatenings; if by despair, then we believe not
his promises.   And justifying faith, though
it principally looketh to the promises of
salvation, yet generally it respecteth the
whole word of God.   The manifold sins,
then, that we see in others, and do commit
ourselves, do apparently shew, how full of
unbelief we and the whole world is ; for if we
did believe God to be true in his threatenings and in his promises, we should be kept
from sin.

Besides, when men are fallen into any
sins, what is the cause that they do not
speedily repent them of them, and so leave

them, but only unbelief? For if they did rightly believe either the promises of God, as, At what time soever a sinner shall return from his sins, and do that which is lawful and right, he shall surely live, and shall not die (Ezek. c. 18, v. 21): all his transgressions, that he hath committed, shall not be remembered, or laid to his charge: they would presently repent, and leave their sins, that they might be forgiven them. Or if they believed his threatenings; as, Kiss the Son, least he be angry; and ye perish in the mid way, when his wrath shall suddenly burn, blessed are all that trust in him (Psal. 2, v. 12): they would speedily repent, whilst mercy is offered; least God take them away before, or bring some great judgment upon them. But contrary to the truth of God's word (according to the nature of unbelief) they imagine some thing of their own head, wherein they rest; and let all men say to the contrary what they will, they will believe none but themselves, and their own conceit.

As that, they shall do well enough though they continue in their sins: or that they shall have time enough hereafter to repent them at their leisure: and that they may

repent them when they list, or some such
like : of which there is nothing promised
in the word of God, but the clean contrary
set down often and very plainly. Therefore that men, when they have fallen into
any sin, do so easily continue in them, and
either repent them not at all, or do it very
slowly, and that doth bewray sufficiently,
how full of unbelief they are.   Seeing
therefore that it is so universally spread
over all men, no marvel if the better sort do
complain so much of it in themselves, and
find it to be a great deal more than they
would.

Again, let us be in trouble, and want
means to help ourselves, and see if we be
not prone to distrust God ? and so not to
depend on his Providence : but rather to
use unlawful means to help ourselves : or
to be too restless and unquiet in the use of
those that are lawful : and so either altogether to forget to seek unto God by prayer :
or else to do it very coldly, and with little
hope.   Though God hath said (Psal. c. 50,
v. 15), Call upon me in thy trouble, so will
I deliver thee, and thou shall glorify me.
And be contented with those things that
ye have, for God hath said, I will not fail
thee, nor forsake thee (Heb. c. 13, v. 6).

And first seek the kingdom of God, and his righteousness, and all things necessary shall be ministered unto you (Heb. c. 6, v. 33): and a thousand such promises more : which doth shew that unbelief possesseth men every manner of way, and there is no man in the world altogether free from it, though it be a great deal more in some than in others.

And to be short, when we are tempted unto any sin, we by lamentable experience find, that we are too easily overcome, because we believe not God's threatenings, that he will assuredly punish it. And when we are tempted for any sin, how soon are we ready to despair, because we believe not the promises of forgiveness unto the repentant? So that this sin is found in the whole course of our life: insomuch that when we have overcome many other sins in the first and second table, then we shall be either wholly overcome with unbelief, or greatly polluted with it.

The Devil did greatly assault our Saviour Christ with this, both in the first entrance into his office, and also in the last discharging of it. First of all in the wilderness, when he would by that long time of abstinence

and want of corporal food by the space of
forty days and forty nights, have persuaded
him, that God had forsaken him, and had
no care of him ; for then he would have
provided for him all this while : and therefore he must now shift for himself, and if he
could do any thing, he must shew his power,
If he be the Son of God indeed, he must
command that these stones be made bread
(Matt. c. 4, v. 3). Secondly, when he was
upon the cross ; for then they that passed
by reviling him, and wagging their heads,
said (chap. 27, v. 39), If thou be the Son
of God, come down from the cross : and
the priests also mocking him, said, He
saved others, but he cannot save himself :
if he be the King of Israel, let him now
come down from the cross. So that they
concluded against him to the weakening of
his faith, that God did not care for him, because he did not presently deliver him.

Thus by tempting him to unbelief in the
beginning, he sought to discourage him
from it ; and by the same temptation of
unbelief in the ending, to cause him to give
it over, before he happily finished it. And
in the same manner the Devil setteth
upon the members of Christ : in the
beginning of their calling, he greatly buf-

feteth them with unbelief, and puts into
them many fears and doubts, that their
sins shall not be pardoned; that so they
might as men tired in the combat, give
over, and return to their old bias. And
before their death he terrifieth them again
with fear, that they shall not go to heaven,
that so in despairing of so great a matter,
they might give over seeking it any longer.
But Christ did overcome by the power of
his Spirit in those temptations of his, that
by the same Spirit he might succour us in
our's. And so in all things he was made
like his brethren, that he might be merciful, and a faithful High Priest to make re-
conciliation for the sins of the people
(Heb. c. 2, v. 17): for in that he suffered,
and was tempted, he is able to succour
them that are tempted. As he did here in
due season help the unbelief of the Apostles, in shewing unto them his hands, and
his feet; but most of all his weak and poor
servant Thomas. For when he had said
(John c. 20, v. 25), Except I see in his
hands the print of the nails, and put my
finger into the print of the nails, and put
my hand into his side, I will not believe:
Then a little after Christ appeared unto
him, and said unto him (ver. 27), Put thy

finger here, and see mine hands; and put
forth thine hand, and put it into my side;
and be not faithless, but faithful.

But to proceed, the first degree of Thomas's unbelief appeareth in this, that he
did hear this often, and of divers that were
very credible, and yet he did not believe it:
as first of all of divers holy and godly
women, and namely (Luke c. 24, v. 10),
of Mary Magdalen, and Joanna, and Mary
the mother of James, and other women
with them, who early in the morning returning from the sepulchre, told the eleven that Christ was risen; and also he
heard it again of Cleopas, and another Dis-
ciple (ver. 33), who told them they had
seen him, and spoken with him after his
resurrection; and now the third time he
heard it of all his fellow Apostles, being
ten in number, all of them very credible,
who did avouch it unto him upon their own
knowledge, and said that they had seen
him themselves. It was appointed in the
equity of the law, that in the mouth of two
witnesses, or at the mouth of three witnesses, every matter should be established
(Deut. c. 19, v. 15). Therefore there was
no colour to discredit so many witnesses,

especially coming in to testify the same
truth at several times. But herein appeareth the nature of infidelity, which is, to
cause us, though we hear the truth of God
witnessed unto us by sundry men, and at
divers times, not to believe any one of them
in divers things, but only ourselves. And
though they be never so grave and reverend,
and constant in avouching of it, and sound
in proving of it, yet all shall be as we
think, and say ourselves, and not otherwise: and thus they are wiser in their own
conceit, than seven men that can render a
reason (Prov. c. 26, v. 16). Whereby it
cometh to pass, that they hinder themselves
in their salvation: for though God send his
servants unto them, to tell them his will,
they will believe nothing, but as they conceive themselves.

And this, though it be a great sin, yet
it was not proper unto Thomas only, but
it was found in the rest of the Apostles at
this present. And that we might not
wonder at it in them without any profit, we
shall see it as deeply rooted in ourselves,
and others: for this is but a looking-glass
to let us see our own unbelief in. For
how often have we heard one and the same
truth constantly delivered unto us by the

Prophets, Evangelists, and Apostles? and yet we do not believe them: we have sundry times heard them, and read them, yea they have been often preached unto us, and that by sundry of the faithful ministers and servants of God; and yet we give no credit unto them: and this is too true, whether we look to God's fearful threatenings, or his merciful promises, both for this life, and the life to come.

How oftentimes, and by how many men have we heard, that unless we repent, we shall all perish; and yet very few believe it, for they go on still in their sin, and think that they shall do well enough. And that every tree, that bringeth not forth good fruit, shall be hewn down, and cast into the fire (Mat. c. 3, v. 10): that is, all wicked ones, that will not speedily amend their lives, shall be cast into hell fire: and yet though they live never so wickedly, they think to be saved, as well as the rest. And though a sinner do evil an hundred times, and God prolong his days, yet it shall not go well with him at the last (Eccles. c. 8, v. 12); yet men think the contrary, that seeing they have escaped in one sin unpunished, and the second and third time, that therefore it shall go well with them for ever : and they think, as the Prophet saith (Psal. 50, v. 21), that because God holds his tongue, he is like them, and liketh their ways well enough.

Moreover, how often have we heard, and by how many, that he that is angry with his brother unadvisedly, is culpable of judgment (Mat. c. 5, v. 22) : and whosoever hateth his brother is a manslayer (1 John, c. 3, v. 19) : and yet men nourish these evil affections in themselves, as though these sayings were utterly false. And hath it not often been sounded in our ears by men of great credit, That neither adulterers, nor fornicators shall inherit the kingdom of God (1 Cor. c. 6, v. 9) : but yet I would to God that the wicked lives of too many did not sufficiently bewray the thoughts of their hearts, namely, that they did not only somewhat doubt of the truth of this, but they think it to be a mere fable : and let men say what they will against these sins, they will believe none but themselves : so wholly are their hearts possessed with infidelity.

Yea let a man come, and deal with one in any sin of his, in which he is settled, and denounce the judgments of God against him out of the truth of his word : and let a second and a third man likewise preach the same unto him at another time : and he yet is resolute in himself, he knoweth as much of that matter as any man can tell him, he will believe none but his own deceitful heart, and his own feeling ; unless he feels the smart of it upon himself, he will give no credit unto it : like unto the men of Sodom, who when righteous Lot told them of fire and brimstone that should come down from heaven upon them for their horrible wickedness, they judged him to be an old doting fool (Genesis c. 19, v. 14), and would not believe it until they saw it, and felt it themselves burning about their ears, when it was too late.

By this infidelity, which is in us naturally, we are enemies to our own salvation, in that we will not believe this part of God's holy word, preached unto us often by them that are worthy of all credit. And this was the state of all of us, till God of his great mercy did reform us, and purge us of this unbelief, that for the amendment of our lives, and repenting us of our sins, that we might be saved, we would believe nothing of God's judgments, and of hell fire, though preached by many ; but only such things as our blind reason did persuade our false hearts of: and that we did stick fast unto, whatsoever men said, and of never so many, to the contrary. And the same unbelief remaineth still in us in measure in that part that is unregenerate.

We must therefore examine ourselves, that we may find it out, and pray to God to help us against it, which no doubt he will, if we seek unto him and be desirous to be holpen of it; as he did here his servant Thomas the Apostle. For this story of his unbelief is written to comfort all those that are fallen into unbelief, and are desirous to be rid of it and to believe, as this Apostle was. But if men for want of due examination and trial of their own heart, do presume of that which is not in them, and so imagine that they believe when they do not, or to have more faith than they have; they shall one day find that their phantasy hath deceived them, and they shall be far from being holpen in that which they want. For many think that it is the easiest thing in the world to believe, when as indeed it is the hardest; and it is more hard to overcome our reason in believing, than the affections of our heart in doing: and therefore Christ saith (Mat. c. 7, v. 14), The gate is strait, and the way narrow that leadeth unto life, and few there be that find it.

And that which hath been said of God's judgments, it is true also of his promises, that there is as much unbelief in us towards the one, as towards the other. For how often have we read the same sweet and comfortable promises of God made for our good: yea how often have they been preached over and over again unto us; and yet we either not believe them at all, or not as we should. Let us take one for example. The Lord saith by his Prophet (Psal. 50, v. 15), Call upon me in the day of thy trouble, so I will deliver thee: and whosoever shall call on the name of the Lord shall be saved (Joel c. 2, v. 22). Yet when trouble and affliction cometh, oh how few do believe this to be true! as appeareth by their practice; for how few, or none at all almost, do seek unto the Lord by earnest and fervent prayer! and they that do, with how little confidence and hope of being heard do they practise it! which sheweth how full of unbelief they are.

Few or none can say, as Solomon doth (Prov. c. 18, v. 10), that the word of the Lord is their strong tower, and that they run to that, as to their sure defence: or as

David taught the people to say (Psal. 20, v. 7), Some trust in chariots, and some in horses, but we remember the name of the Lord our God; that this is the first thing that they remember, as that which shall do them most good. But prayer is either so wholly neglected, or men come to it so slowly, as it were drawing their legs after them, and last of all, as though they did not one whit believe the promises this way made unto them.

Nay, which is more, if any come to them in their trouble, and tell them that they have often found this to be true by experience in themselves, as David doth (Psal. 34, v. 6), This poor man cried, and the Lord heard him, and saved him out of all his troubles : yet we do not believe that we shall find it to be true in ourselves. Especially if God defer us any while, we can give no credit to the truth of his promises, until we see them verified in ourselves : but we are ready to say, unless we see and feel these things in ourselves, we will not believe it.

Again, how often, and by how many, have we heard this truth of God, All things work together for the best unto them that love God (Rom. c. 8, v. 28) : that is, God

will turn all the afflictions of his people
unto their good in the end: yet when the
least cross doth befall us, how are we dis-
mayed, as though this were false, because
we do not believe it! And if any shall
then say unto us, be of good comfort, bear
it patiently, the Lord herein seeketh your
good, and you shall come out of this affliction better than you were before; yet we
think it a matter impossible; yea, a mere
fable: and that it is better for us to be
otherwise, and so we will not believe him;
nor others, though they should come im-
mediately, and tell us the same upon good
trial, that they found it to be so in themselves, as David saith (Psal. 119, v. 71), It
is good for me that I have been afflicted,
that I may learn thy statutes: and before
I was afflicted I went astray, but now I
keep thy word (Psal. 66); and as the
Apostle Paul also saith upon his own experience, and the rest of the faithful in whose
name he speaketh, We know, that all
things work together for the best unto
them that fear God (Rom. c. 8, v. 28).
Not only I myself, but many others also,
do know this to be true. Which is as if a
skilful physician should say unto his sick
patient—take this potion, though it be

bitter it is for your health, I have found
the proof of it by long experience: nay
not only I myself, but all we physicians do
know it to be so: and yet the patient
would believe none of them, but himself.
Oh what a great root of infidelity is within
us! how had we need to strive against it!

To be short, how often have we heard
this promise of our Saviour Christ; First
seek the kingdom of God, and his righteousness, and all outward things shall be
ministered unto you (Mat. c. 6, v. 33):
and that also of the Apostle Paul unto
Timothy, Godliness is profitable unto all
things, which hath the promise of this life,
and of that which is to come (1 Tim. 4, v. 8):
yet let us be in any want, and it is a wonder
to see how hardly or not at all we with
cheerfulness depend upon God's Providence, until such time as we can see how to
provide for ourselves. Let other men
come and say what they will, and what
they have found by experience in themselves and in others, concerning the truth
of this, we do not almost regard it, or take
any comfort in it: so full of unbelief are we,
and so common a thing is it, in the matters
of God, to give credit to none but to our-

selves : as the Apostle St. Thomas saith of himself here.

Lastly, let us come to the matter of our salvation : if Satan the accuser of the brethren (Rev. c. 12, v. 10), and our own conscience do set before our eyes the remembrance of our sins, and press us somewhat therewith ; though we be heartily sorry for them, and do weep bitterly, as Peter did at the remembrance of his fall (Mat. c. 26, v. 75), and do wish a thousand times that we had never committed them, and thus travel and groan under the heavy burthen of them, as that which is able to press us down unto the bottom of hell, and unfeignedly turn from them unto God, saying with David (Psal. 51, v. 1), Have mercy upon me, O God, according to thy loving kindness : according to the multitude of thy compassions put away mine iniquities : yet how hard a matter is it then to find that in our hearts which we say with our mouth, I believe the forgiveness of my sins ; especially in the day of temptation, and in the hour of death : though we have oftentimes before heard the blessed saying of the Apostle (1 Tim. c. 1, v. 15), This is a true saying, and by all means worthy to be received, that Christ Jesus came into the

world to save sinners : and that comfortable voice of our Saviour Christ (Mat. c. 11,
v. 28), Come unto me all ye that are
weary and laden, and I will ease you.

This then we see is no new thing, for
men not to believe sundry parts of God's
word brought unto them by the ministry
of divers of his faithful servants, by reason
of the great unbelief and hardness of heart
that is in them : whereby it cometh to
pass that their own understanding doth
more prevail with them to distrust, than
the testimony of many to believe. How
then had we need to find out this unbelief
in ourselves : which when we have done,
we are not to judge too hardly of ourselves,
seeing that it is so common, but only la-
ment and bewail it, and seek unto Christ
to be holpen of it, who is the author and
finisher of our faith (Heb. c. 12, v. 2) : and
say with the Apostles, Lord increase our
faith (Luke c. 17, v. 5) : and with the man
in the Gospel, Lord I believe, help my unbelief (c. 9, v. 24).

And if there be such great streams of unbelief in God's children, till they be holpen
of it, what a bottomless sea, think you, is
there of it in the wicked ? whereby it
cometh to pass, that they are filled with all

atheism and profaneness; casting the word of God behind their backs, so that let never so many learned and godly men witness the truth unto them for their amendment, they will believe no more than they have determined beforehand with themselves. Let us pray to God for them, that they may have better minds, even desirous to believe; and then shall they be holpen in time, as the Apostle St. Thomas was. And for ourselves, let us labour to have teachable hearts, that we may reverence and give credit unto them who in the mystery of our salvation know more than we do, and have in the matter of faith a great deal more experience than we ourselves. That so it may come to pass, of what mind soever we have been before, that when God's faithful servants whom we should esteem and trust, they shall tell us so and so, whether for God's judgments, or for his promises, or for the direction of our lives, we may believe and obey them. Then shall we come to faith, and be confirmed in it (Prov. c. 10, v. 17): for he that regardeth instruction, is in the way of life.

And if in other matters we think it reasonable, that we should believe those that have more knowledge than ourselves; yea

even clean contrary to that we thought
before: as for the matter of our health we
believe many skilful physicians for the state
of our bodies, and many expert lawyers for
the state of our lands and goods; why
should we not then in matters of divinity,
and for the state of our souls, give more
credit to many skilful divines than to ourselves? Especially whenas the general
rule holdeth as well in that as in any other
science, that every skilful man is to be
credited in his own art and faculty: our
reason is more corrupt in this, than in any
other thing, and therefore there is more
cause that we should believe others than
ourselves.

Therefore, as in other matters, when we
are doubtful, we confer with them that
have more skill and knowledge, and give
credit unto them contrary to our own
thoughts, and we are ready to rely upon
them rather than upon ourselves: so let us
do in matters of faith, and let us not offer
God's servants and ourselves this great
wrong, that we will believe all men in
other things, saving than in this. It is too
much, that we have done it so often already,
let us not continue in it—that we should
come to the Church, and hear God's word,

preached, and go away not believing it:
and come again the next day, and then depart away as full of unbelief as before:
and thus from day to day, and so still be of
this mind, that whatsoever men say, we
will believe none but ourselves, thinking
that we have reason as well as they, and
therefore, unless we can conceive it by reason,
we will not admit it, whatsoever they say.

For faith is above reason, therefore we
must believe the servants of God in things
whereof we can conceive no reason: nay
reason is against faith, and there is nothing in us more to hinder us from
believing, than to hearken to our own
reason. For the natural man (by his
best reason) perceiveth not the things of
the Spirit of God, for they are foolishness unto him: neither can he know them
(by his own wit), because they are spiritually discerned (1 Cor. c. 2, v. 14): that is,
by a supernatural enlightning of the Spirit of
God. So that matters of faith we cannot only
not by reason comprehend them, but they
seem foolishness unto all them that will no
further give credit unto things than they be
demonstrated by reason: which made the
Apostles, when the women came from the
sepulchre, and told them that Christ was

risen, not only not to believe them, but that
their words seemed unto them as a feigned
thing, and a mere fable that had no truth in
it (Luke c. 24, v. 11): and therefore Christ
saith in the Gospel (Mat. c. 16, v. 24), If any
man will follow me, let him forsake himself, that is, his own reason most of all, that
so he may believe others contrary unto it.

And this is that which is so highly commended by the Spirit of God in our Father
Abraham (Rom. c. 4, v. 18), that he above
all hope (that reason could afford him)
believed under hope, that he should be the
father of many nations: for he considered
not his own body, which was now dead,
(that is, void of strength, and unmeet to
get children,) being almost an hundred
years old: neither the deadness of Sarah's
womb: neither did he doubt of the promise of God through unbelief; but was
strengthened in faith, and gave glory to
God, being fully assured that he that had
promised it, was able to do it: where we
see, that renouncing his own reason, which
would have held him in unbelief, he rested
upon the truth and power of God, and so
believed above that by reason could be
shewed him, or he able to conceive: and
so must we do also.

E

The Apostle saith (Heb. c. 11, v. 3), that through faith we understand that the world was ordained by the word of God, and that the things which we see, are not made of things which did appear: that is, that this great and beautiful frame of the world was made of nothing, is a matter not to be comprehended by any reason, but only by faith: which made not only the Epicures, but also some of the wisest philosophers to hold, that the world was eternal: for it was unto them a principle in reason, that of nothing comes nothing, neither can you so multiply nothing, that there should come any thing of it.   Therefore the Apostle saith, that he that will hold that all these things, which we see in heaven and earth, were made of nothing, he must believe it above all reason.

And who can by any reason conceive the truth of this article of our faith, The resurrection of the body? that is, that these very bodies of our's, being turned into dust and ashes, the same in every part and member should be raised up again. Some of the wiser sort of the Heathen did acknowledge the immortality of the soul, and that there was a place of joy for them that lived well, and of pain for them that swerved from the rules of right reason, after death. But that the same bodies of men should rise again, they did not so much as once dream of it, because they could not comprehend it by any reason: therefore in that matter we must believe others above all reason.

The like is to be said of alms, which hath a promise of increase: so that by giving to the poor we shall not lose any thing, but gain: which is a thing contrary to reason, that the more a man should give away from himself, the more he should enrich himself: and therefore few do believe it, which maketh them covetous and hard-hearted, and to be willing to depart from nothing, lest they should want themselves: and especially to be most hard-hearted to their poor brethren in the times of scarcity and want, when they should be most liberal, and by that means best provide for themselves: which St. Paul was so fully persuaded of, that he doth commend it unto us by an excellent comparison, saying (2 Cor. c. 6, v. 9), He which soweth sparingly, shall reap also sparingly: and he that soweth liberally, shall reap also liberally. Where he compareth alms unto sowing of seed: the more a man soweth, the more he reapeth by God's blessing: the more a man giveth, the more he receiveth by God's promise : the one we see by experience, which maketh men in the times of dearth and scarcity to sow most : the other we comprehend by faith, which maketh the believer, in the hardest times, to be most liberal. Thus we see what unbelief is in us, in that we give no credit unto others any further than we can conceive a reason of it : which is the same that was in St. Thomas : and yet he was cured of it; and so may we by the same grace of God, if we will learn this lesson — that in the time of temptation we believe others above ourselves : which if we do not, it is the next way to remain in unbelief for ever : but if we can come unto this, there is hope of us in time.

THE second degree of Thomas's unbelief, appears in this ;—that he would not only not believe this, being thus often told him, divers times, and by sundry credible persons, but he will believe none but himself : for he saith in plain words, Except I see in his hands the print of the nails, I will not believe it. Which is, as if he had said, you indeed tell me that you have seen Christ risen again, and so do divers others; I have heard these things often ; but I have not yet seen him myself; what others have seen, that appertains not unto me, unless I see him myself I will not believe it. This therefore is further to be considered, because sometimes it falls out, that there is good cause why we should not believe a thing spoken often and by many.

And if they be of any good credit, though there be no cause in truth to suspect them, yet it may seem unto us that there is some : and hereupon it cometh to pass, that some in their unbelief take exception against the preachers, and think that they have some cause why they should not believe them in the things that they have preached unto them, though in truth there be none. But yet to be altogether of this mind that St. Thomas was here in this matter, that we will believe none in the world but ourselves, that seemeth to be such a thing as wanteth all colour of reason. And yet thus unreasonable is unbelief, as we see most clearly in this example : for he saith very peremptorily, that unless I myself do see in his hands the print of the nails, I will not believe it. He doth not say, unless better men than you do tell me so; or unless I hear more in number; or unless I hear better reason for

this matter than I do yet, I will not believe it : but if all men in the world tell me
of it never so often, unless I see him mine
own self, I will believe none of them : which
is as if he had said, In this case I will believe myself, and nobody else.

We see then whither unbelief will drive
us if we give place to it, even that we shall
believe none but ourselves. And indeed so
it is in all sorts in whom it reigneth, they
will believe no more from any man than
they can persuade themselves by their own
reason : unto that they obstinately stick
against all men : and so are not ashamed to
say, I will believe none of you all ; I will
believe mine own self, and further I will not
be led by any : no man shall draw me to
believe that which mine own reason tells
me not. And thus they so much abound
in their own sense through unbelief, that
they persuade themselves that they have
more reason for that they hold, than all
other men have for the contrary.

And so let men say never so much against
that which they have conceived themselves,
they still imagine that they have some-
thing to say against it, and some reason
why they should not believe them. And
this is most true, not only in matters of

faith, but for life and conversation : which
is the cause both that Papists and other
heretics are so obstinately addicted to their
errors, and also wicked men so altogether
wedded unto their sins, that neither the
one nor the other can be reclaimed from
them.   And therefore when men have said
what they can, they will not give them
over, for they have determined to believe
none but themselves : and of this mind
will they be, till God rid them of their unbelief: and then the saying of Christ shall
be verified upon them, Blessed are they,
that have not seen, and have believed (John
c. 20, v. 29): that is, they shall believe
others besides themselves, and so blessed
shall they be: as indeed this is the way to
faith, and so to blessedness, to distrust ourselves, and to believe the servants of God,
speaking unto us in his name : of whom
Christ hath said (Mat. c. 10, v. 40), he
that receiveth you, and your doctrine, receiveth me.

And that we might come unto this, we
are to remember, that true faith yields unto
the bare word of God against our own reason ; and so giveth glory unto God, as the
Apostle saith (Rom. c. 4, v. 20), acknowledging, and reverencing his truth, mercy,

and power, where we can see no reason of it, and so praising him for the same, and resting in it. Which we see to be true in Abraham, not only in the birth of Isaac, which was beyond the course of nature, and so above all reason : but also in the offering up of the said Isaac his son, whom he loved, and in whom he received the promises, even that with him God would establish his covenant, and with his seed after him for ever (Gen. c. 17, v. 11) : and therefore take away him, and take away all, and the hope of all : and yet at the commandment of God he was contented to offer him up for a burnt offering in mount Moriah (c. 22, v. 10) : which he did by faith, as the Apostle saith : for he considered that God was able to raise him up even from the dead (Heb. c. 11, v. 19) : and so he measured the performances of the promises of God, not by his own reason, though never so great, but by the truth and power of God.

The like may be said of Noah concerning the building of the Ark, of whom it is said (ver. 17), that by faith he being warned of God of the things which were not as yet seen, moved with reverence, prepared the ark to the saving of his household. In which matter if he had consulted with flesh and blood, and conferred with his own reason, he should never have undertaken so great a matter. For how could he thereby imagine that all the world should be drowned except his family, and that they should be saved, and all the rest perish: when by the space of 120 years, he both preparing the ark and preaching their destruction, not oné man or woman would believe it besides his own family of eight persons; might not he have thought that he was deceived rather than they all? And how could he have hope that four men should govern so great a vessel, wherein should be male and female at the least of every living thing upon the earth and in the air, with sufficient provision for them all for the space of an whole year; and that not in the great ocean sea, but when the whole world was a sea? And where could he think to have means to take and bring in all these fowls of the heaven, and beasts of the earth? and how could they attend upon them all to feed them, and to do all things necessary unto them? And many more things might be put into his head, to cause him to desist from this work, as a thing impossible; and no doubt he was subject unto many of these, and such like temptations, but the Apostle sheweth us, how he overcame them all, even by faith : whose nature and property is, to rely upon the commandment and promise of God above all reason, and contrary unto it.

But on the other side unbelief, which is contrary unto faith, that resteth wholly and only upon reason ; insomuch that, unless they can see some reason how that may be done that is said and promised, they will not believe it, they think it impossible, they reject it as an unreasonable thing. A most lively pattern whereof we have in that great man of Samaria, in the days of Ahab king of Israel, at what time by reason of the siege of the king of Aram, there was such an extreme famine, that women did eat their own children (2 Kings c. 6, v. 28). Then the prophet Elisha did prophesy unto them great plenty on the sudden, even the next day following. To whom this great prince, on whose hand the king leaned, answered and said (c. 7, v. 2), Though the Lord would make windows in heaven, could this thing come to pass ? as though he had said, this is impossible, though the Lord shall rain down corn from heaven among us : for

he could not conceive by any reason, how
either the siege should be so suddenly
raised; or if it were, how it should come to
pass, that corn being so unreasonably dear
to-day, it should be so exceedingly cheap
to-morrow. But God verified his own word
unto them at the time appointed, and this
man saw it with his eyes, but never tasted
of it, because of his unbelief. For the king
appointed him to be governor, and to sit
in the gate of the city, to see the corn sold
to the people, who so thronged, that they
trod upon him, and there he died (ver. 20).

The whole world is full of this unbelief,
that they will believe no more than their
own reason persuades them unto : and that
which goeth against their reason they are
ready to cross it, though it be never so true.
For how many are there, that have set
down with themselves, that whatsoever the
preachers say, they have determined a
course, which they think they have good
reason for : in that they mind to continue;
beyond that they will not go; they are so
settled, that out of it they will not be re-
moved; they hope they are not now to
learn; they are too old to be taught; they
trust that they have not lived so long for
nothing; they have wit and reason as well as

other men; and so that which they have
conceived they will stick unto, that course
they have entered into they purpose to
continue in, and in that they mind to live
and die; and this course they hold for
doctrine both of faith and manners, for du-
ties to God and to men; and thus they
will believe none but themselves, and their
own reason.

And thus, though they come to the
church from day to day, they come not to
learn any thing, they have determined beforehand what they mean to do. They
will learn of no man, they can teach themselves sufficiently. Whereupon it cometh
to pass, that though they daily hear their
sins rebuked, they will amend nothing;
and the judgments of God denounced
against them, they will believe nothing:
they think they have better reason for
their doings, than any man can have
against them. And if they be called upon
to increase in knowledge and godliness, and
so to go on to perfection; they stand still
at a stay, and think it not necessary; they
like well of their own doings, and no man
shall remove them from them; they will
believe none but themselves: unless I see

reason for it mine own self, I will not believe you.

Thus through unbelief the word is choaked in the greatest part of the hearers, as our Saviour Christ sheweth in the parable of the seed: and it profiteth them not one whit, no more than it did the Jews when it was preached unto them, because it was not mixed with faith in them that heard it (Acts c. 4, v. 2). And so that is the very cause, why in this long time of preaching, there hath been so little good done, even the great unbelief that reigneth in men every where. Of which the prophet Isaiah had too great experience in his time in them to whom he preached, and doth with great grief complain of it, when he crieth out thus pathetically, who will believe our report? and to whom is the arm of the Lord revealed? (Isa. c. 53, 1): meaning, that none would believe it, but those whose hearts God touched by his holy Spirit. And thus by their doings men do too apparently shew, that though they do not utter it with their mouths, yet they say it with their hearts, that let men say what they will, because as they think they have some reason against it, they will believe none but themselves.

F

Let us labour to see this unbelief in ourselves in any measure that we have it, and be sorry for it, and strive against it: and pray God to forgive us, and help us. And that we might this way be holpen, let us not be too much addicted to our reason, and measure things by it: for our natural reason being corrupt, it doth not only not further us unto faith, but doth sometimes hinder us from it; not only because faith is of things above reason, but contrary unto it. Therefore in the matter of our salvation we must be so far from being addicted to our own will and reason, as that we must utterly deny it, that we might believe: as the Apostle St. Thomas should have done here: and have said, though this that you tell me be a matter impossible in mine understanding and reason, and I cannot possibly conceive how it should be: yet because so many of you being of conscience to speak the truth, I believe it.

And thus did Abraham concerning the promise which God had made unto him (Rom. c. 4, v. 20): for it is said, that he did not despise or reason against the promise of God through unbelief: where these two are joined together as subordinate, and

come helping one the other, namely, reason and unbelief, and not reason and faith.
So that if we hearken to reason, it will
cause us to doubt rather than believe: and
the next way to believe, is not to listen or
give credit unto the disputes and doubts
that reason will minister unto us. For it
is able to object many things against that
which we should believe; and therefore if
we will be Christ's disciples, we must deny
not only all our sinful affections that might
draw us from obeying his doctrine, but our
reason especially, which might dissuade
from believing it. That when our reason
shall tell us one thing, as that we may continue in our sins a while longer, we may
repent at leisure, and be saved well enough:
and that the way to heaven is not so strait
as men speak of: and then we shall hear
the contrary out of God's word daily, we
must believe that contrary to our reason,
if we will be saved. For Thomas remain-
ing in this unbelief, he might have perished
for ever, but that Christ had mercy on him
extraordinarily, and yielded unto his unbelief for the good of the Church; that for
his sake, he might shew himself unto his
Apostles after his resurrection another time.
Therefore first of all let us pray to God

to sanctify our reason, and to enlighten it
by his holy Spirit, that we may be capable
of the mysteries of the word of God: as
David doth, Open mine eyes, that I may
see the wonders of thy law (Psal. 119, v. 18).
And secondly, when we come to hear and
read the word of God, let us bring these
minds with us, that what reason soever we
seemed to have for our opinions and doings
before, when we shall hear the contrary
avouched by the servants of God, and
proved out of the Scripture, we give them
over, and credit them above ourselves. And
let us renounce that reason of our's, that
shall minister unto us any thing against
that which hath been taught us ont of the
Scripture, and not hearken unto it. For if
we should hold the Angels of God accursed,
if they deliver any thing to us contrary to
the written word of God (Gal. c. 1, v. 8);
then much more should we accurse and
deny our own reason, that should suggest
any thing unto us contrary to the same: and
let us not after so long time of preaching
be still of this mind, that we will believe
none but ourselves.

A THIRD degree of the unbelief of St. Tho-
màs appeareth in this, that he saith, Except

I see in his hands the print of the nails, and put my finger into the print of the nails, and put my hand into his side, I will not believe it. For, as though it had not been sufficient that he had said, that he would believe none of them; nor any other that should tell him as much as they did: he would believe none but himself: he further addeth, that unless he might see in his hands and feet the print of the nails, and put in his finger into them, he would not believe it. Which is as if he had said, if I may not only see himself, as you say you have done; but may be sure of it, and therefore may also see in his body these marks that he had on the cross, and especially if I may come so near unto him that I may feel them, and put my finger into them, I will believe it; otherwise I will not. So that he will no further believe, for all their sayings, than his outward senses shall persuade him; and namely, his sight and feeling: if I may see and feel, I will believe, and till then I will not believe.

Oh, wonderful infidelity: especially in one that was so near Christ, and had been so long time conversant with him. For what if Christ had never appeared unto him, nor unto any other of the Apostles : was it not sufficient unto them, that he had often before in their hearing said, that he should be put to death, and the third day rise again (Mat. c. 16, v. 31, c. 17, v. 9, and c. 26, v. 32): and that they were charged to shew no man that vision which they saw upon the mountain, until he was risen again from the dead: and after I am risen again, I will go before you into Galilee? Should they not have been left without excuse in their unbelief? Seeing they had heard it from his own mouth so often before his death: and now after his resurrection divers credible women did tell them that they had seen him risen again, according as he had often told them.

Besides, if he were of that mind, and thought that he had good reason for it, that he would not believe, unless he did thus see and feel him, why may not other be of the same mind too? and so Christ should have remained upon the earth unto this day, and not have ascended into heaven: or else often since he should have descended to shew himself to those that should believe: if none would believe further than they should see and feel. Moreover after that he had thus seen him and felt him himself, would he not have thought it strange, if others would not have believed him, when he preached unto them the resurrection of Christ? why then doth he make such a straight rule to himself?

Surely, that in him we might see a pattern of that great weakness that is in us, and how full of unbelief we be: and a lively example of the great mercy of Christ in bearing with sinners in the same: and by all means putting them out of the same in time, that they might be saved.

And why doth he say thus rather than any thing else, Except I may see and feel, &c.? Are these two senses such sure judges of the truth that they cannot be deceived? May not a man think that he seeth and feeleth that which he doth not? and may he not again doubt, whether he seeth and feeleth that which indeed he doth? How came it to pass that when Elisha had caused water to come miraculously into a valley of the wilderness, for the Kings of Israel, of Judah, and of Edom, that the Moabites when as early in the morning the sun rose upon the water, and they saw the water as red as blood over against them, they said, This is blood: the kings are surely slain, and one hath smitten another: but when they came

to the host of Israel they found it otherwise. And as the sight of these men deceived them, so did the feeling of Isaac deceive him in his old age. For his son Jacob
coming unto him in the person and habit
of his elder brother Esau to receive the
blessing: when he felt the roughness of his
neck and hands, which Rebeckah had covered with skins, he judged by his feeling
that it was Esau. For he said, Come near,
my son, that I may feel thee, whether
thou be my son Esau or no; and when he
had felt him he said, The hands are the
hands of Esau.

Thus we see that sight and feeling may
easily be deceived: and yet this is the nature of unbelief, to give credit more unto
these deceivable senses, than to many other
things that are more sure and certain.
And many men in matters of faith will
almost believe nothing, until such time as
they see and feel them: and therefore
when they are taught what in heaven is
prepared for them that serve God; what in
hell for them that disobey him; they are
ready to say, who hath seen them? giving
us to understand, that they will not believe
them until they either see them, or feel
them themselves. Was not this unbelief

universally spread over the face of the
whole world before the flood, when Noah
the preacher of righteousness declared unto
them the judgment of God that should
come upon them for their sins; and namely,
that God would bring a flood of waters upon
the earth to destroy all flesh wherein was
the breath of life under the heaven, because all flesh had corrupted his way, and
the earth was filled with cruelty; and thus
he continued preaching 120 years: but
none of them believed it, though they saw
him also all this while preparing the ark for
the saving of himself and his family. And
therefore they continued still in their im-
penitence, and in their sins, till the flood
came and took them all away. And so
they said to Noah, some in their thoughts,
some in their words, as Thomas did here in
another case to the Apostles: You say that
the world shall be drowned, but except we
see the rain come in such measure, and
feel it, we will not believe it.

And was not the like infidelity afterwards
in all the men of Sodom, where just Lot
lived, and was vexed with their uncleanly
conversation: for which he denounced
God's judgment against them: and at the
last by special revelation of the Angels that

were sent unto them, he said unto his sons-in-law which had married his daughters, Arise, go out of this place, for the Lord will destroy this city; but he seemed to his sons-in-law as though he had mocked. Thus they would not believe it, because they saw it not, nor any likelihood of it, till fire and brimstone came down from heaven, and fell upon them, and consumed them. And so they being condemned, and the city overthrown, they were made an example unto them that after should live ungodly, and which would not believe the truth of God's judgments against sin in the mouths of his servants any further than they shall see and feel themselves.

' Thus we see how common this is among all unbelievers, so far as infidelity prevaileth with them, that they will believe nothing that is threatened against sin any further than they see and feel it themselves. When in the famine of Samaria there was exceeding great plenty against the next day promised by Elisha the Prophet, did not one of the Princes say, when I see it, I will believe it, and not before. Whereupon this answer was given unto him, Behold, thou shalt see it with thine eyes, but thou shalt not eat thereof. And

so unbelief discredits not only the threatenings, but the promises, except they can
see them with their eyes, and feel them
with their hands : of which we shall speak
more afterwards,

Doth not St. Peter say, that there
shall come mockers in these last days,
which will walk after their lust, and say,
where is the promise of his coming ? for
since the fathers died, all things continue
alike from the beginning of the creation.
Wherein he sheweth how men through unbelief will make a mock of Christ's second
coming, and of the end of the world, and of
the day of judgment : because with their
eyes they do not see any such thing likely
to come to pass : when they shall see some
great alteration in heaven and in earth
bending that way, they will believe it, and
no sooner, nor any further.

And we find by experience the truth of
this daily in many, that they will believe
nothing of this matter any further than they
can see themselves. And our Saviour Christ
in the Gospel hath foretold and forewarned
us of this, when as he saith (Luke c. 17, v. 26),
As it was in the days of Noah, so shall it be
in the days of the Son of Man : they eat,
they drank, they bought, they sold, they

married wives, and gave in marriage, unto
the day that Noah went into the ark, and
the flood came and destroyed them all.

Likewise also, as it was in the days of
Lot, they ate, they drank, they planted,
they built: but in the day that Lot went
out of Sodom, it rained fire and brimstone
from heaven, and destroyed them all : after
these ensamples shall it be, when the Son
of Man shall be revealed : that is, not only
it shall come suddenly and all things shall
continue in their ordinary course : but men
shall then give themselves to all pleasure
and worldliness : and shall neither believe
it, nor think of it, till it come: as the
men of the old world did not : of whom
the Evangelist St. Matthew saith, that they
knew nothing, till the flood came and took
them all away : so shall also the coming of
the Son of Man be.   They knew nothing,
not that they had not heard of it, for Noah
did preach unto them an 120 years before :
but they did not believe it, nor regard it,
because they saw it not : even so shall it be
towards the end of the world : though they
have heard of these things an hundred
times, yet they will know nothing till they
see it.

And not only this sin reigneth in the

wicked, that they will believe no more of the promises and threatenings; of the joys of heaven, and pains of hell, than they can see and feel themselves: and so because they do neither of them yet, they will believe none of them, let men say what they will, and never so long; and so they go on in their sins, and live thereafter; which is greatly to be lamented. But also if we will examine ourselves and other men, we shall find, that this was in ourselves and in them, till the Lord had mercy upon us: That though we had often heard that God was just, and would punish sin, yet we presumed otherwise, and did not believe it, because we escaped a while in our sins, and did not see and feel the truth of it in ourselves; and by that means went on, and were hardened in our sins. And so that was verified in us, as well as in others, which the Lord complaineth of by his Prophet, These things hast thou done, and I held my tongue: therefore thou thoughtest that I was like thee: but I will reprove thee, and set them in order before thee (Psal. 50, v. 21).

And thus not only before our calling, infidelity did wholly bear the sway in us, but also since that time a great remnant of it

still remaineth in us : so that in many
things we will believe no further than we
see and feel, especially in the time of
temptation : for if we be in any great trouble, and then if there be a messenger of
God sent unto us Job, or an interpreter
of his word, one of a thousand, as Elihu
calleth him, who shall bid us be of good
comfort, and put our trust in God, he
will help us and deliver us in his good
time ; and declare unto us many promises
of his word to that end : we then, if we
want means to help ourselves, we are ready
to say, O but I see not how and which
way that should be. So that if we did
presently enjoy the promised help that we
might feel it, or had means to bring it to
pass that we might see it, we say we would
believe it, or else not. So our faith goeth
no farther to comfort us than our senses of
seeing and feeling. And this is too true
in what affliction soever we be, either of
poverty, sickness, or any other distress.

And this unbelief of our's is so much the
more dangerous and the more deeply rooted
in us, because though we have had experience of God's goodness towards ourselves
in time past, wherein we may remember
how he hath holpen and delivered us

beyond all that we could foresee, or have any hope of; yet at another time we trust him and his word no further than we can see ourselves. Thus the people of Israel doubted of the power of God, whether he would give them flesh in-the wilderness according to their desire, though they had seen his power before in giving them water out of the hard rock: whereof David speaketh after this manner (Psal. 78, v. 18), They tempted God in their hearts, in requiring meat for their lust: they spake against God also, saying, Can God prepare a table in the wilderness? Behold, he smote the rock, that the water gushed out, and the streams overflowed: can he give bread also? or prepare flesh for his people? Where he aggravateth their sin of infidelity, in that they seeing before how he beyond all hope brought water plentifully out of the rock to supply their want, they did now doubt that they should have no flesh, though Moses had promised it unto them from God, because they could not see how in the wildnerness such abundance should be prepared for so great a people, that every one might have enough.

And we ourselves are subject to the like, not only in these outward things, and are therein too much misled, because we rely

wholly upon our outward senses ; but also
in the matter of our salvation, therein our
unbelief doth especially shew itself, so that
we can hardly or not at all believe any
thing beyond our sense and feeling.   For
when we are humbled under the weighty
hand of God with the sight of our corruption and sins, and have the feeling of God's
wrath upon us for them in any measure ;
then, though we hear the comfortable promises of the Gospel made to all that unfeignedly turn from them : As there is no
condemnation to them, that are in Christ
Jesus, which walk not after the flesh, but
after the spirit (Rom. c. 8, v. 1): and If
you will inwardly wash and make your-
selves clean from them, and take away the
evil of your works from before your eyes ;
cease to do evil, and learn to do good :
though your sins were as crimson, they
shall be made white as snow : though
they were red as scarlet, they shall be as
white as wool (Isaiah c. 1, v. 16) : that is,
if you leave them, I am ready to forgive
them, though they be never so many : and
then we find by the grace of God, that we
utterly detest them, and are weary of them,
as of an importable burthen, and have cast
them away from us, as a filthy cloth : yet
because we see not the light of God's

countenance shining clearly upon us, and have not the feeling of his love poured into our hearts, we cannot believe the pardon of them as we ought. And unto all the promises that are brought for our comfort, we are ready to object: alas, we have no feeling of that which is said unto us. Which is as if we should thus speak: you say thus and thus unto me, but I can have no comfort in it; for unless I see it and feel it, I will not believe it. Which unbelief, though it be very great, yet Christ Jesus doth bear with them a while in it, and help them of it in due season, as he did his servant Thomas the Apostle here.

And truly as the Devil did by God's permission thus far prevail with the Apostle St. Thomas that he was brought to this strait, that without seeing and feeling he would not believe; so with this one temptation of his he hath so mightily prevailed against many of the best servants of God, that he hath brought them to a very low ebb, even almost to their wits' end. For besides that he hath driven them to this extremity, which is very great, that they will believe no more of God's favour towards them than they can see and feel in themselves; he hath gained this also at their hands, which is much more: that because they have no feeling, therefore they say they have no faith: as though these two were both one, feeling and faith; or as though they were always necessarily joined together.

And hereupon have come the great complaints and outcries, which some of them have made against themselves in the time of their trouble: and not only of those who have grossly and apparently fallen into some sin, and therefore there was some manifest cause of it, but of those also which have lived blamelessly, neither have been tainted with any great sin: and yet both of them in the time of their temptation have uttered many bitter words against themselves; as that they are altogether out of the favour of God; that they are not in the number of them that shall be saved; they have no part in Christ; they are none of God's children; and such like. And why so? for say they, they have no sight and feeling of their favour of God in themselves, and therefore they have no faith, neither can have; for except they have some feeling in their hearts, they cannot believe.

And this temptation hath lien upon the conscience of some more heavily, and of others less: upon some longer, upon others shorter time: even as it hath pleased the Lord either in wisdom to try the one, or in mercy to succour the other.   This was that which did so oppress David, as appear-eth in many Psalms, that he was almost in despair of himself: when he said (Psal. 13, v. 1), How long wilt thou forget me, for ever? how long wilt thou hide thy face from me? and will the Lord absent him-self for ever? and will he shew no more favour?. is his mercy clean gone for ever? and doth his promise fail for evermore? hath God forgotten to be merciful? and hath he shut up his tender mercy in dis-pleasure? (Psal. 77, v. 7): and, My God, my God, why hast thou forsaken me? and art so far from my health, and from the voice of my roaring?   I cry by day, but thou hearest not; and by night, but have no audience (Psal. 22, v. 1)... And thus he continued, till it pleased God for our in-struction and comfort to give him victory; partly by considering the former merciful dealing of God towards himself and others; partly by meditating upon the constant truth of his promises, which made him at the last trust unto him, and depend upon him without any present help or feeling.

And thus he endeth the 38th Psalm, which
he made to put himself in remembrance of
some great affliction of God that was upon
him, and therefore entitles it a *Psalm of
Remembrance :* in which are many grievous complaints both of his sins, and of the
punishment of them, without any feeling
of present help and comfort; only he
saith (ver. 15), that he would wait upon
God, hoping that he would shew himself
favourable in time, though he had no present feeling of it.   And so must we do in
the like case.   But in the mean season we
see, that this measure of unbelief that was
in the Apostle St. Thomas, that he would
believe no more than he could see and
feel, is and hath been in others also, and
that all of us are subject unto it more
or less.

But that we may arm ourselves sufficiently against this grievous temptation, and
comfortably support ourselves when we
shall fall into it, we must consider that faith
and feeling are not only not all one, nor
always joined together, but also that they
are many times severed in the children of
God ; so that there is faith, where there is
not nor can be any present feeling : yea,
that the greatest faith sometimes is, where

there is no feeling at all. And to this end
we must remember what the Apostle saith
of the nature of faith, It is the ground of
things which are hoped for, and the evi-
dence of things which are not seen (Heb.
c. 11, v. 1). Where, he saith, that faith is
of such things as we see not, and of those
things which are but hoped for, and we as
yet have not the present possession and
feeling of them, and yet we believe them.
And this he proveth by most excellent ex-
amples, when as first of all he addeth
(ver. 3), Through faith we understand that
the world was ordained by the word of
God : so that the things which we see are
not made of things which did appear : that
is, we know by faith, that the whole world
was made of nothing, and this verily we
believe : but who did, or ever could see
this ? Therefore we do, and must believe
that which we have not, neither can see ;
and so we have the knowledge of it by
faith, and not by sight.

Secondly, he thus speaketh there of the
faith of Noah (ver. 7), that he being warned
of God of the things which were as yet not
seen, moved with reverence, prepared the
ark to the saving of his household. Where
two things are noted, he believed that

which he could not see.: 1st. that all the world should be drowned for their sins; 2dly, that by repentance and faith himself had found favour with God, and should be saved in the waters: and therefore he made the ark according to God's commandment long before he saw the flood, or any token of it, that he might be saved in it. And so he believed the judgment of God to come upon the wicked, and salvation promised to himself, though he could not see, nor have any present feeling of either of them. And this is that operation of faith which it must have in us; even to cause us to believe both the threatenings of God's judgments against impenitent sinners, and the promises of salvation to them that walk before him in truth, though we have no present sight or feeling either of the one or of the other. For we must consider the constant truth of God's word, both in his justice and mercy, which in time shall be verified, though for the present there be no visible signs and tokens thereof to be seen or felt of ourselves, or any other.

The third example is of Sarah, the mother of us all: of whom it is said (ver. 11), that through faith she received strength to conceive seed, and was delivered of a child,

when she was past age, because she judged
him faithful which had promised. When
a man-child was first promised unto her,
being both old and barren ; as long as she
measured things by sight and feeling, she
believed not this, neither could : For she
saw, that it ceased to be with her after the
manner of women, therefore she laughed at
it within herself, as at a thing impossible
(Gen. c. 18, v. 11) : for which she was re-
proved with these words, Shall any thing
be hard to the Lord? But when she gave
over consulting with reason, she believed
not only without, but clean contrary to all
sense and feeling : for she looked only to
this, that he was just and true who had
promised it unto her ; and by this faith
was made fruitful. So in matters of faith
we must not look to what we see and feel in
ourselves, or in any means to effect them ;
but what God hath promised, and how
faithful he is to perform.

And so did Abraham, of whom it is
written (Gen. c. 15, v. 5), that the Lord
brought him forth, and said, Look up now
to heaven, and tell the stars, if thou be able
to number them : and he said unto him,
So shall thy seed be : and Abraham believed
the Lord. And the Apostle commendeth

this faith in him so much the more, because he considered not his own body,
which was now dead; (that is, void of
strength and vigour to get children), being
almost an hundred years old: neither the
deadness of Sarah's womb, who was both
aged and barren (Rom. c. 4, v. 19). Both
which if he had looked unto, he could have
had no sight or feeling of that which was
promised; for they were directly against it.
But he gave this glory to God (ver. 20),
that he was fully assured, that he that had
promised it, was able to do it: and so
above hope, he believed under hope, that
he should be the father of many nations,
according to that which was spoken unto
him, So shall thy seed be. And so he believed that which he neither had, nor
could have any present sight or feeling of.

Thus both Abraham and Sarah believed
that which they could have no feeling of in
themselves; and so must all the sons of
Abraham, and daughters of Sarah. And
thus to do is not only faith, but the greatest faith. For if they could have seen how
this might have been been done, and have
felt such strength in their bodies, that they
might perceive it very likely by the course
of nature; then it had been no great matter.

to believe it: nay it had been great infidelity not to believe it. So for us to believe the promises of God, when we may see and feel how they may be performed, that is a matter of no moment; but when all things go against them, and we have no sight or feeling at all in ourselves of that which is said unto us; then to believe God, and to give this glory unto him that he is able to perform it, is a matter of great faith. And therefore here it is said of Abraham, not only that he believed, but that he was not weak in faith (ver. 19): that is, very strong and constant in faith. So that the Spirit of God commendeth this in him, as an high degree of faith, that he believed without sight or feeling; to shew us that faith is so many times severed from feeling, that it is then the strongest, when we constantly believe that, which we neither see nor feel, but wait upon God for them both.

And this is that which was in our Saviour Christ also: who though he did always put his trust in his father, and was sure that he loved him; and his faith this way was as precious and pure as gold; yet it did most of all shew itself in his full strength, when he came to suffer upon the cross : when it was so many ways assaulted, that contrary to all sense and feeling he remained constant, and so overcame ; to succour all those that shall be oppressed with the temptations of unbelief, because they have no feeling. For when things did lie so heavy upon him, he being then to bear all our sins and corruptions, and in them to appear before God his Father, and to answer for them, yea to satisfy his wrath by enduring the full punishment of them ; first of all it is written of him (Mat. c. 26, v. 37), that he began to wax sorrowful, and grievously troubled in his mind : and this grief was so deadly, that he was not able to contain it in himself, but did bewray it with the most lamentable words unto his Disciples, that he might have comfort from them ; saying (ver. 38), My soul is very heavy unto the death, tarry ye here, and watch with me : and then because his grief was not assuaged, he fell upon his face down to the ground, and prayed, saying (ver. 39), O my father, if it be possible, let this cup pass from me. And thus he prayed the second and third time. And that it might appear what uncomfortable striving he had in himself all this while, not only with death, but with

the fearful judgment of his angry Father,
it is further added (Luke c. 22, v. 44), that
he fell into a great agony and distraction of
mind, whereby all his body was distempered, so that for anguish his sweat was
like drops of blood trickling down to the
cold ground.

And at the last when he was upon the
cross, he was further assaulted with temptations from the speeches of men, even his
enemies, which reviled him (Mat. c. 27,
v. 39), wagging their heads, and casting
out many opprobrious speeches against
him, saying (ver. 40), If thou be the Son of
God, come down from the cross: he trusted
in God, let him deliver him, if he will
have him : for he said, I am the Son of
God. Whereby his discomforts and discouragements for our sakes were so in-
creased, that at the last he burst forth into
these most lamentable words (ver. 46), and
as the Evangelist saith, straining as it were
all the parts of his body, and powers of
his spirit, he cried with a loud voice, My
God, my God, why hast thou forsaken
me? All this while what present sight
and feeling could he have of God's favour ?
when as not only all things outwardly did

shew, but his words also did abundantly declare, that inwardly he felt the contrary.

Therefore his faith was now the greatest,
as it was meet it should be, to encounter
and overcome so many and great temptations: when as contrary to all these things
which he saw and felt, he not only prayed
most earnestly unto his father, and continued therein praying three times the same
words, with such fervency of spirit that
being upon the cold ground he sweat
water and blood; and he prayed in faith
(Heb. c. 5, v. 7): For when he did offer
up those prayers and supplications with
strong crying and tears unto him that was
able to save him from death, he was heard
in the thing which he feared; and God
sent an Angel unto him from heaven to
comfort him (Luke c. 22, v. 43). Whereby
he came to this resolution of mind, that he
quietly submitted himself in these his sufferings unto the will of his father; saying
(Mark c. 14, v. 36), Abba, Father, all
things are possible unto thee: take away
this cup from me: nevertheless, not that I
will, but that thou wilt be done. And
being now at the point of death, and in the
midst of all his sufferings, and in the height
of his temptations, that it might appear

that he had overcome all, he cried out with
a loud voice, straining himself to the utter-
most when life was almost out of his weak
and painful body, Father, into thine hands
I commend my spirit (Luke c. 23, v. 46);
and when he thus had said, he gave up the
ghost, and quietly died. Which words of
his being uttered with great zeal, did shew
the excellency and perfection of his faith;
especially if we consider in what case he
was then: and so his faith was the greatest,
when he had the least feeling.

And thus no doubt the servants of God
in their several afflictions of body and
mind, and otherwise, are in measure made
like unto Christ: when as having nothing,
that by any sight or feeling inward or outward, might minister unto them any comfort, and therefore in such cases they are
greatly discouraged and cast down in themselves; yet they hold out constantly in
them to the end: then the more like they
are unto Christ in his sufferings, the more
like shall they be unto him in his glory.
For then is their faith the greatest, when
in this forlorn estate of their's (as it may
seem) they can pray unto God as Christ
did, and seek for all help and comfort from
him: and never leave praying till God hear

them, · as Christ continued in his prayer till an Angel was sent unto him. And in the mean time whatsoever becomes of them, they with a quiet and meek spirit resign up themselves wholly to his blessed will, being contented whatsoever they desire, that not their own but God's will may take place: as Christ did when he said, Father, not mine, but thy will be done.

And if they do so, that if affliction present, of what nature and kind soever, shall make an end of them, they can quietly and peaceably commend their souls and bodies, even themselves wholly living and dying into his blessed hands; as Christ did also upon the cross, when he was ready to give up the ghost; being persuaded that nothing ever perished that was committed into his custody: according as he saith himself (John c. 17, v. 12), Those that thou gavest me have I kept, and none of them is lost, but the child of perdition; that the Scripture might be fulfilled. If we can thus do, though all this while we have no feeling of any present comfort, yet it may be truly said unto us as it was to the woman of Canaan, who with many discouragements and without all sight or feeling of any favour from him, pursued our Saviour Christ with her prayers, and would not give over or take any repulse, O woman great is thy faith (Mat. c. 15, v. 28) : and, O man, great is thy faith, that doest thus, whosoever thou art.

And we have a worthy example of the truth of this in one of the Martyrs of our own country, and in the memory of man, as it is largely set out by Mr. Fox in his laborious work of the Acts and Monuments of the Church. The effect of which story shortly is this :—Mr. Robert Glover, of Coventry, gentleman, and Master of Arts in Cambridge, was in the reign of Queen Mary, with many the servants of God, by the malicious practices of the Papists apprehended, and brought before the Bishop of the diocese for his faith and religion, and after examination he was sent to prison ; where he received great comfort from the Lord from time to time ; and as his afflictions did increase, so did the comforts of the Lord abound; till at the last by the permission of God, for his further trial and comfort, the Devil did greatly assault him in prison by the consideration of his unworthiness to be counted in the number of those that should suffer for Christ's sake ; which temptation of the enemy, though he did constantly resist at the first, yet after that he was condemned to death by the bishop, and was at the point to be delivered out of this world, it so happened that two or three days before the time of his burning, his heart being lumpish, and destitute of all spiritual consolation and feeling of God's favour, he felt in himself no aptness or willingness, but rather an heaviness and dulness of spirit, full of much discomfort to bear that bitter cross of martyrdom, ready now to be laid upon him.

Whereupon he fearing himself, least the Lord had utterly withdrawn his wonted favour from him, made his moan to one M. Austen Bernher, a minister, and a familiar friend of his; signifying unto him, how earnestly he had prayed day and night unto the Lord, and yet could receive no motion, nor sense of any comfort from him. Unto whom the said Austen answering again, willed and desired him patiently to wait the Lord's pleasure, and howsoever his present feeling was, yet seeing his cause was just and true, he exhorted him constantly to stick to the same, and play the man: nothing misdoubting, but the Lord in time would visit him, and satisfy his desire with plenty of consolation. Whereof, he said, he was right certain and sure, and therefore desired him whensoever any such feeling of God's heavenly mercies should begin to touch his heart, that then he would shew some signification thereof, whereby he might witness with him the same; and so departed from him.

The next day, when the time came of his martyrdom, as he was going to the place, and was now come to the sight of the stake; although all the night before praying earnestly to God for strength and courage, he could find none, neither had any sight or taste of the favour of God in himself, suddenly he was so mightily replenished with God's holy comfort and heavenly joys, that he could not smother it in himself, but cried out, clapping his hands to Austen, and saying on this wise, Austen he is come! he is come! &c. and that with such joy and alacrity, as one seeming rather to be risen from some deadly danger, to liberty of life, than one passing out of this world by any pains of death. Here we see that great was his faith, when he was willing to give his body to be burnt for the testimony of Christ, and was now going to the stake to that end, though he had no feeling of God's favour then by any joys that he felt in himself. He could never have suffered thus for the truth, if he had no faith: if then he had died in this case without the sense of any special comfort, he must needs have died in the faith of Christ for which he did suffer: and so he should have had faith, yea very great faith, not only living, but dying without any sense or feeling.

But I will come unto another example, which though it be far more ancient in time, yet it is better known unto us, as being recorded in the holy Scripture. The patience of Job as it is set down as a pattern, and commended to all men to follow, so none can doubt of his faith also but that it was very great, when he is thus numbered among the faithfullest men that have lived upon the face of the earth. When the land sinneth against me by committing a trespass, then will I stretch out mine hand upon it; and though these three men, Noah, Daniel, and Job, were among them, they should deliver but their own souls by their righteousness, saith the Lord God (Exod. c. 14, v. 13). When all that misery came upon him, that we read of in the Scripture (Job c. 1, v. 3), as that in one day he lost seven thousand sheep, three thousand camels, five hundred yoke of oxen, five hundred she-asses: and all his sons and daughters died a violent death after a strange manner; and in his own body he was smitten with sore boils from the sole of his foot unto the crown of his head; and he being in this pitiful case, all friends did forsake him; yea they that were younger than he did mock him, and they whose fathers he refused to set with the dogs of his flocks (c. 30, v. 1): and his men-servants and maids took him as a stranger, and though he called them, they would not answer him; though he prayed them with his mouth: and his breath was strange unto his wife, though he prayed her for the children's sake of her own body (c. 10, v. 16): and three of his principal friends did set themselves against him, and by their reasoning did greatly discourage him, as though he had been an hypocrite all the days of his life; and that his holiness of life was but in shew, and not in truth: and he had no rest neither night nor day, for when he laid himself down, he said, When shall I arise (c. 7, v. 4): and so measuring the evening, he was weary with tossing to and from, unto the dawning of the day. Neither was he quiet waking nor sleeping:

tell them the contrary, they would not
believe them, neither could they possibly
doubt of it, their sight and feeling did sufficiently instruct them. But when the
clouds shall cover it, or in the night both
the light and heat thereof shall be taken
away, then to be fully persuaded that the
sun is still in the heavens, and that it hath
lost nothing of the light and heat of it;
that is a matter of a deeper conceit, and
more experience.

Even so when the testimonies of God's
favour and love are so many and great, and
so plentifully upon us both outwardly and
inwardly that they may easily be seen and
felt, then to believe that God is gracious
unto us, and to be persuaded of his favour
towards us, is that which the weakest in
faith may attain unto without any diffi-
culty; but when all these shall be taken
away, not only in our own judgment, but
in the opinion also of others. and the light
of God's countenance shall be as it were
darkened with the clouds of adversity, and
all things outwardly shall be as uncomfortable unto us as the darkest night of
winter; yet then to believe that God is
one and the same towards us, and that his
love suffereth no eclipse at all, but is the

same still to us, and to all those that are his, because whom he once loveth, he loveth unto the end, and that the gifts and calling of God are. without repentance (Rom. c. 11, v. 29): and that all the paths of the Lord are mercy and truth, unto those that keep his covenant, and his testimonies (Psal. 25, v. 50): that is, that he is not only merciful unto them in the beginning, but also true and constant in his mercies towards all his even unto the ending, to finish and make perfect in them that good work of his, that he hath begun in them. For he is not like unto man that he should repent him of any thing that he hath done (1 Sam. c. 15, v. 29): and as St. James saith (James c. 1, v. 17), with him there is no variableness, or shadow of turning. To be, I say, thus persuaded, when these things shall be upon us, and so to rest in the truth of God's promises, and to wait patiently for a comfortable feeling of the performance of them in ourselves, is a matter of greater faith, and of longer experience.

Again, as if a man doth come into a fruitful garden or orchard, well set with many trees in the spring time, when all things are green and blossom, or in

summer, when the trees are full of fruit, it
is the easiest thing in the world then even
at the first sight to be persuaded that the
trees are living and growing; and he that
hath the weakest senses, and meanest wit,
and least experience, is able to say so: but
to come thither in the depth of winter,
when all the fruit shall be gathered, and
the leaves fallen, and see all the boughs
white with the hoar frost, and rine hanging
upon every twig, so that outwardly they
seem to be dead and rotten; yet then to be
persuaded, that they are living, and that
the sap is at the root, which in time will
come into all the branches again, and
shew itself as before in putting forth
leaves, blossoms, and fruit; this requireth
better judgment, and more experience.

So it is in the matter of faith: when all
the testimonies of God's love do abundantly
shew themselves, as it were, in summer, it
is an easy matter to believe: but when all
these shall be fallen away from us, as they
were from Job, and there is a very hard
and long winter full of many storms come
upon us; yet then not to be too much
discouraged and cast down, as though all
were clean lost and gone, but to be persuaded that the favour of God is not clean

dried up, but is at the root, that is, is the same in Christ towards us that ever it was; and that as the Apostle saith (Heb. c. 13, v. 6), Jesus Christ is yesterday, and to-day, and will be the same for ever: and that the light of God's countenance is not clean put out, but darkened, and covered with a veil for a time; and so with a quiet and meek spirit to wait upon God in all well-doing, till there be a new spring, and till the sun break out of the clouds again. Thus to do, is that great faith that shall uphold us in all extremities. And as in these cases we would condemn others of want of wisdom, which would believe no more than they saw or felt, so must we condemn ourselves and others of want of spiritual and heavenly wisdom of the word of God, that in such cases as these of our salvation, we will believe no more than we can see and feel: and we must commend the other to be of better judgment and greater faith, who do believe more than they could either see or feel.

For the relieving of ourselves therefore in such cases as these, what must we do? We must do that, which Thomas the Apostle should have done: namely, he should have believed those that told him,

that Christ was risen, and that they had
seen him : and he should have believed
the words of Christ himself, who had foretold him, that he should be put to death,
and that within three days he should rise
again : which words of Christ must needs
have been verified in their time, though
none had ever seen him. So must we do,
even believe the word and promises of God
in the mouths of his faithful servants, who
are able both to see further into them, and
also to discern more testimonies of faith
and of the favour of God in us, than we
ourselves can do. And though we, whom
they do most of all concern, do not see
them at all or as we desire : it is sufficient
that others, whom we ought to credit, do
see them in us, and do constantly and upon
their credit avouch the same unto us.

For it is most certain and true, though
every man should best know himself, yet
it so often falleth out that we are not fit
judges of ourselves, and of our own estate,
neither of body nor of soul : and therefore
if we will be rightly persuaded of ourselves,
we must not so much rely upon our own
judgment, as give credit unto others
who may and do see that in us, which we
ourselves do not, neither can. As when a

man is dangerously sick of some disease,
though he have some general knowledge of
the estate of his body, yet he may take
himself to be stronger or weaker, nearer or
farther off from death, than indeed he is:
and therefore in such case we ask the ad-
vice of some skilful physicians, and trust
their judgment better than our own; insomuch that though a man be a very skilful
physician, he will hardly or not at all practise upon himself in great extremities, but
useth the help of other physicians, and is
contented to be ordered at their discretion:
even so when a man is dangerously sick in
his soul, either of unbelief, or otherwise,
he is not to judge of himself at that time
though he be a very good Christian, but he
must for his recovery out of that estate,
use the help of other godly ministers, and
hearken unto their judgment concerning
himself.

And that we might see the truth of this
most clearly in another case, we must consider, that as when the Devil prevaileth
against us by presumption, we so favour
ourselves, and are so partial that way,
that we imagine, both that we have those
virtues and graces of God in us and that
in great measure, which we have not,

neither can any man see them in us ; and also that we are free from those corruptions and sins, which yet do apparently break out in us, and all the world may easily see them : so on the other side, when he hath gotten the advantage of us by diffidence and despair, he maketh us too rigorous and hard against ourselves, and persuadeth us that we want those graces which do apparently shew themselves to others ; and to have those sins and corruptions, and that measure of them which in truth we have not, neither is any able to discern them in us, though we cry out against ourselves for them.

So that in both these estates, wherein we deceive ourselves of ourselves, if we will be holpen, we must deny ourselves, and not measure our ourselves by ourselves, but give credit to those, who as they are wise to discern and faithful to judge, so are they also true to report what they think of us and of our estate. Which if we will not do, we must needs continue in our unbelief and other sins so much the longer ; and it shall be a very hard thing to recover us out of the same. Let us therefore, as we love our own good, in such extreme cases as these, when by the temptation of

Satan we are brought to a narrow point,
hearken unto those faithful ministers and
godly brethren of our's, who are able (because they are out of temptation, and the
case is not their own), better to judge of
us than we ourselves : and then have we
made a good entrance unto the curing of
our souls, though we be not presently
restored to perfect health; and though we
have not present comfort, yet the extremities of our fears shall be greatly stayed : and
this staying of us will minister further hope of
full recovery ; and it is none of the least
mercies of God to see, that we have been deceived in ourselves, and are not able rightly
to judge of ourselves. Thus we see how
faith and great faith, is without feeling :
and when we be oppressed with this temptation, how we must help ourselves by believing others more than ourselves, yea
even of our ownselves.

Moreover, to this effect must we be ad-
monished, that as in the natural life there
are three ages, the infancy, the childhood
or youth, and the riper and perfect age ;
so in the spiritual life the Scripture maketh
mention of three ages; for of those that
are in Christ, and truly belong unto him,
some are new-born-babes, as St. Peter

calleth them (1 Peter, c. 2, v. 2), but newly begotten of the immortal seed of the word of God : others are little children, that have more profited in knowledge, and in the mystery of their salvation (Gal. c. 4, v. 19) ; and some are in comparison of them, perfect men, and are coming unto the measure of their full age in Christ (Eph. c, 4, v. 15). These latter are able to judge of themselves, and of others ; for by long custom they have their wits exercised to discern both good and evil (Heb. c. 5, v. 14) : the second sort is less able to judge of themselves ; the third not at all. A babe though it be heir apparent unto the crown of the greatest monarch in the world, it hath no sense or feeling of it : nay, though it liveth, it is not able to judge of itself, whether it hath life or no : but others do see by the operations of life, that it is a living creature, and hath an immortal soul : and dying in that estate, yea as soon as it is born, it shall hereafter live for ever and ever.

So a great many that are born again of water and of the spirit, and thereby are made heirs of the kingdom of God, as Christ saith to Nicodemus (John c. 3, v. 5) ; they are never but babes ; beyond that age

they never go, and some of them fall asleep
in the Lord, as soon as they are made par-
takers of this spiritual birth ; as the thief
upon the cross died presently after his con-
version : and Christ sheweth us in the
Gospel, that some are called at the eleventh
hour to work in the vineyard (Mat. c. 20,
v. 6), that is, in the latter part of their life
they are called to the state of salvation and
grace, and to receive the reward of their
calling, which is eternal life. In which
estate of theirs they can have little or no
feeling at all of their spiritual life. But as
other children die before they know that
they were alive, so these die before they
did feel any great power of the spiritual
life in themselves. But as others did see
that it was alive, because they saw how it
desired the milk of their mothers, and how
they did thrive by it; so others may see in
such spiritual infants, that the life of God
is in them by the appetite that they have
unto the word of God, that they esteem it
as their appointed food, as Job saith of
himself.(Job c. 23, v. 12), and that thereby
they grow in many graces of the Spirit of
God, as in a fear to offend him, and in a
desire unto their own salvation, though
they have little assurance, sense, or feeling

of it in themselves : and so are heirs of the kingdom of God, though they die before ever they had any great feeling of it in themselves.

And for those that are of riper age in Christ, and have had some feeling of their salvation, and have lost it ; they are not to be addicted to their own judgment, to think they never had it because it is now lost, or that they shall never have it again because it is taken from them for a while ; for the life of God may still be in them, though the present feeling of it be taken away ; and therefore at this time, concern- ing their own present state, they must be- lieve others, that can see more into them than themselves. For as in some diseases of the body a man may have all his senses taken away from him for, a while ; or he may be so sore wounded in the head, and his brain so distempered, that he cannot tell whether himself be alive or dead ; but others by their breathing, and some other operations of life do see evidently that life remaineth in them, and so hope that they may be recovered ; so a man may be so spiritually sick of unbelief, or so sore wounded in his soul with temptations, that he cannot see any token of God's favour in

4

himself; but yet by the prayers that he maketh unto God to be holpen out of these distresses, by the love that he beareth unto God, and to God's people, and other operations of the Spirit of God in him, they that are wise shall be able to discern that the life of God's Spirit breatheth in them, to whom they must give credit above themselves; and so think that they are in a better state of salvation, than they can see themselves to be.

And it must not seem strange unto us, that others should see better into our estate than we ourselves can. For oftentimes it falleth out, that some great affection of the mind so blindeth us, that we imagine that we have not that which indeed we have. He that is blinded with covetousness of these worldly goods, by the unsatiable desire that is in him, never satisfied, though he hath more to live on than many hundreds, yet still he is complaining of his want and poverty; and saith, that he hath nothing: and tell him of this and of that, which God hath bestowed upon him, yet because he hath not all that he desireth, he maketh no account of them, and all is unto him as though he had nothing. So, he that is sick of a spiritual covetuousness,

and desireth the feeling of God's favour in
a great measure, and such an assurance of
his salvation as might be without all doubt,
which because he cannot come unto, because the flesh lusteth against the spirit,
and in it there is nothing but doubting, he
imagineth that because there is some want
of assurance and feeling, that therefore
there is no feeling at all : as the covetous
man by reason of some want, saith that he
hath nothing : the want of that which he
hath not, so blindeth his eyes, that he cannot see that which he hath : so the want of
some assurance so troubleth them, and they
have so great a desire unto more, that they
cannot see that they have, but for want of
some, deny all.

A remedy against which temptation is,
not to deceive ourselves any longer with an
imagination of such a measure of assurance
of salvation ordinarily in the children of
God, which should be without all wavering
or doubting ; or such a measure of feeling
of the love of God, and joy therein, as
should abandon all distrustfulness and sor-
row ; this is not to be looked for in this
world : the fulness of joy is in the presence
of God, and at his right hand only are
pleasures for evermore (Psal. 16, v. 11).

Here we have them but in measure; there indeed is joy unspeakable, and most glorious, without any interruption; when we shall see God face to face (1 Cor. c. 13, v. 12); and know him as we are known, whom now we behold as through a glass, and so may sometimes doubt whether we see him or no. This measure we must be contented with, and so pray as the Psalmist doth (Psal. 106, v. 4, 5), Remember me, O Lord, with the favour of thy people, that I may see the felicity of thy chosen: where he desireth not such joy and feeling of the favour of God which he did imagine himself, but that which God doth usually bestow upon his people, which is that which is joined with much doubting, and many fears, even then sometimes when it is at the best; and so not imagine, that unless we have it according to our own desire, we have it not at all, or as God's people use to have it. For undoubtedly it is thus with the best, at one time or other.

And concerning this desire of feeling and assurance, we must understand thus much, that none can have this, but those that believe: so that though we should want them both altogether, yet the desire that we have unto them, doth manifestly

argue that we have faith. For who can desire to feel the heat and light of the sun,
but he that hath life in him ? a dead car-
case cannot do it. So if there were not the
life of the Spirit in us by faith, we could
not have any desire to feel the favour of
God in us in truth at all. He that is never
so weak, yet if he still desire strength, it
appeareth that there is life in him : so
when we most earnestly desire to be
strengthened in the assurance of our salvation, it is a manifest token, that the life of
God is still in us : therefore let us comfort
ourselves with such desires, and know assuredly, that as they be of God, so he will
satisfy them in his good time : for the
Lord heareth the desire of the poor, he
prepareth their heart, and bendeth his care
unto them (Psal. 10, v. 17) : that is, as he
giveth them so earnestly to desire these
things, which others neglect, so he will
shew, by giving also that which they do desire, that he hath not given them such holy
desires in vain. For the saying of our
Saviour Christ must be verified upon all
men, without respect of persons, Blessed
are all they that hunger and thirst, not
only after righteousness, but after any
other graces of his Spirit, for they shall be

satisfied and filled (Mat. c. 5, v. 6). And the saying of the Virgin Mary shall be verified in them, He hath filled the hungry with good things, and sent away the rich empty (Luke c. 1, v. 53); that is, as they that have no such desires, can look for no such feeling, so they that are unsatiable in their desires that way, shall be satisfied in time with abundance of feeling; and if they wait upon God with patience believing these promises, it shall be unto them according to their faith.

That I might not say here that, which is yet most true, that while they so unmeasureably desire it, they have it in a good measure. For herein is the saying of St. Augustine most true, that the desire of any grace of God, is in some sort the grace itself. He that unfeignedly desireth the forgiveness of his sins, doth with this desire obtain the remission of them. He that desireth a greater measure of repentance, doth from day to day profit in repentance: he that desireth not to sin, is no sinner before God: he that desireth the favour of God, hath obtained it already: he that desireth the assurance of his salvation, and the feeling of God's favour, he hath both of them in some sort already,

When Abraham was willing to offer up his son Isaac at God's commandment, he is said to have done it by faith (Heb. c. 11, v. 17): his desire before God was as though he had done it: so when we offer up these desires unto God, it is as well with us in his account, as though we had the things themselves.

For as the Apostle speaketh of alms (2 Cor. c. 8, v. 12), if there be first a willing mind, it is accepted according to that a man hath, and not according to that a man hath not: that is, God looketh not so much to his deed, as to his desire; as the poor widow that offered but two mites, was more accepted of God, and commended by Christ, than they that offered much, because of her great desire. So when in the sacrifice of prayer we offer up our hearts unto God with holy desires either for assurance of his favour, or feeling of our salvation, we are accepted of him, as though we had them: and when he giveth us this desire, he beginneth to work the grace itself: and that desire is the earnest penny and pledge of the thing itself.

Christ saith in the Gospel, that whosoever looketh on a woman to lust after her, hath committed adultery with her already in his heart (Mat. c. 5, v. 27). So that the desire unto any sin, is the sin itself before God ; then the desire unto any virtue, is the virtue and grace itself before God. And therefore he that looketh up unto God with an earnest desire of his salvation, he hath obtained it already before God, who seeth and alloweth the desire of his heart. He that looketh on his own unbelief and corruptions with a desire to be rid of them, he is thereby discharged of them before God. Thus we see, that to desire feeling is an argument of faith, as to desire meat is an argument of life ; yea to desire feeling is the very beginning of it in ourselves : and therefore we must be comforted over them.

Concerning which feelings, we must also consider, that in them that have them in the greatest measure, they are not always alike ; but they are going and coming, as the day and the night. And as in the course of nature there is not one tenour of things, but God's works are subject to many changes ; so is it in the course of God's grace : that which we have received, doth not always continue alike, neither have we the same feeling of it to-day that we had yesterday ; whether we look to the

fervency of prayer, or zeal to God's word,
or love to his Saints, or assurance of our
salvation.   Here we must comfort ourselves
with the remembrance of that which we
have found in ourselves in times past, and
hope that we may find the like again : and
say as it is in the Psalm (77, v. 11, and
119, v. 52), I have remembered the times
past, and have been comforted,   For as the
woman that is quickened with child, and
feeleth it stir in her body, though she do
not always feel it stir alike, and sometimes
not at all, and sometimes more weakly than
before ; yet she assures herself that the
child is living, because she hath felt it stir
before, and so hopeth that she shall do
again.   So when Christ is formed in us
first of all, as the Apostle speaketh (Gal.
c. 4, v. 19), we have the feeling of him
stirring and moving in our hearts by his
holy Spirit dwelling in us ; which lively
motions though we feel not so strongly
moving in us afterwards, or not at all ; yet
we doubt not, but that Christ dwelleth in
our hearts by faith still (Eph. c. 3, v. 17),
and hope to feel it as sensibly again in
time, as we have done : and so much the
more, because Christ being formed in us,
never dieth; and therefore the remembrance

of our former feelings must comfort us over
the want of them for the time present; for
they are not always alike in any that have
them: it is sufficient that we have had
them; therefore if we labour after them,
they will return unto us again, when it
shall please God. And thus much for this,
that St. Thomas in this matter of faith ad-
dicts himself to his own feeling.

THE fourth and last degree of his unbelief appeareth in this, Except I see in his
hands the print of the nails, and in his side
the print of the spear, I will not believe it.
For why should he desire this? not only
to see him, and to feel him, but to see in
his hands the print of the nails, and to put
his finger into them; and to see in his side
the print of the spear, and to put his hand
into it. Did he not know that these
wounds and scars were proper unto his
body only while it was subject unto infirmity and weakness; and that after his
resurrection his body was glorified? And
so he might have thought, that though
it should be granted unto him to see him,
yet he could not by any reason or ground
from the Scripture, have hope to see him
thus: and yet he saith, Except I see the

print of the nails, &c. I will not believe it : he doth not say, Except I see him; but, except I see him with the print of the nails, and of the spear, I will not believe it.

This is then the nature of unbelief, that when it will not profit by the ordinary means that God hath appointed for the confirming of faith; it desireth such things, whereof there is no warrant either from reason or from Scripture. As here St. Thomas neglecting what Christ had said unto him, that when he should be put to death, within three days he would rise again: and that also which was told him by the Apostles, and divers others, namely, that he was risen again, and had appeared unto such and such; he saith, Except I see him myself, with the print of the nails in his feet, and of the spear in his side, I will not believe it. Concerning which point, though Christ did rise indeed out of the sepulchre with these marks in his glorified body, and did retain them while he tarried on the earth, that thereby it might more certainly be known, that the same body of his that was crucified, was raised up again; yet Thomas had no general rule to lead him to think that it should be so, but rather according to the common condition of the bodies of all the faithful in the day of resurrection, so to conceive of the body of Christ raised up. For that which is said of the resurrection of all the faithful, the members of Christ's mystical body, must needs be much more true of him the head; for it belongeth to them only by virtue of his resurrection. Now of them the Apostle writeth thus to the Corinthians:—The body is sown in corruption, and raised in incorruption (1 Cor. c. 15, v. 42): that is, with nothing tending thereunto, as wounds do: it is sown in dishonour, having no glory nor beauty on it, as Christ's body was most of all, when besides that the life was gone out of it, and so it looked pale and wan, it had also many deformities by the stripes of his whippings, and the crown of thorns, and the print of the nails in his hands and feet, and of the spear in his side: it is raised in glory; that is, with all perfection and excellency of beauty without any blemish at all: it is sown in weakness, it is raised in power;. and therefore without marks and tokens of weakness and infirmity: for a body sore wounded, even unto death, as Christ was, hath less power in it than it had before. Therefore seeing he desired to see Christ's body raised up, he should not have desired to see it thus, and with these marks.

And for the further confirmation of this, we may remember what the Apostle saith touching the glorious state of our bodies to be raised up: Our conversation is in heaven, from whence also we look for the Saviour, even the Lord Jesus Christ: who shall change our vile body, that it may be fashioned like unto his glorious body, according to the working, whereby he is able even to subdue all things unto himself (Phil. c. 3, v. 20): therefore as we shall be raised up without scars and marks of infirmity, which many have in these days of their pilgrimage; so he had no reason to think but that Christ's body should be. Therefore though he would not believe till he saw him, he could not look to see him, after this manner that he prescribeth.

And though he did at the last appear with these marks in his body both to the eleven first, and afterwards unto Thomas; yet it was not because his body was properly and of its own nature then subject unto them, no more than it was to hunger, when he did eat with them (Luke c. 24, v. 43); but it was by a special extraordinary dispensation; as when Angels that have no bodies, did appear in the shape of men. Therefore this could not be looked for; and it was in respect of the ordinary course of God's dealing somewhat unreasonable to tie the Lord unto that for the strengthening of his faith, and to say, Except I see the print of the nails, and of the spear, I will not believe it: for others had seen him, and not seen him with these; as Mary Magdalen at the sepulchre, where she mistook him to be the gardener, or the keeper of that place, where Christ was buried in a garden (John c. 20, v. 15): and the two Disciples in their journey, as they were going to Emmaus (Mark c. 16, v. 12). Therefore we must take heed how we yield to our unbelief; for it will make us look for and desire such things at the hand of God, for the confirming of our faith, as have no ground either from Scripture, or from reason; though it pleaseth God of his infinite goodness to bear with men sometimes this way, and to yield to them, either to the strengthening of their faith, or to the leaving of them without excuse in their unbelief. So that as the Apostle saith of covetousness, They that will be rich fall into temptation and snares, and into many foolish and noisome lusts, which

drown men in perdition and destruction
(1 Tim. c. 6, v. 9). So we may say of unbelief, that it causeth men to desire many
foolish and unreasonable things, and such
as often tend to their own hurt.

Thus in the Gospel our Saviour Christ, in
the parable of the rich glutton, and in his
person, noteth out the thoughts and desires
of unbelievers here in this world; where
he is brought in speaking unto Abraham
after this manner:—I pray thee Father,
that thou wouldest send Lazarus unto my
father's house (for I have many brethren)
that he may testify unto them, least they
also come into this place of torment (Luke
c. 16, v. 27). Thus unbelievers would
have dead men come from heaven, and tell
them what is done there, and what in hell;
but Christ sheweth what answer Abraham
gave him for our instruction, They have
Moses and the Prophets, let them hear
them (ver. 29): as if he had said, they do
sufficiently declare the truth of these
things, of them they may learn them, and
so it is needless to have any come from
heaven to tell them, there are enough upon
the earth that do declare it daily: and so
do the Apostles and the Evangelists now
much more. But the rich man said again,

Father Abraham, but if one come from the dead, they will amend their lives (ver. 30): which is as if he had said, Though they do hear daily out of the Scripture, what punishment is in hell for the wicked, yet they do not believe it, except some come from the dead, and tell them of it, and then they would.

Thus foolish is unbelief, to neglect the certain testimony of the Prophets and Apostles, which is the ordinary means to reveal his will unto us, and to desire that Angels or dead men might come from heaven or from hell to speak unto them, and then they would believe them ; which in these days is so extraordinary that it is not to be looked for. But this is a short and plain answer for such men set down there from Abraham, who said thus unto him ; If they hear not Moses and the Prophets, neither will they be persuaded, though one rise from the dead again (ver. 31). Where Christ sheweth not only what are the means of knowing these things, even the books of the Prophets and Apostles, in which the will of God is perfectly set down concerning all things that are needful for us to know, and that the other is not to be desired, nor hoped for. So if they had them they would not profit by them, whenas they neglect the other; but yet we see by this, that unbelief is full of these foolish desires.

And truly if we could so well see into the hearts of men, as Christ did when he uttered this parable, we should see, that the greatest part of the world is still of this mind, to neglect all the ordinary means that God hath appointed either to work faith in them at the first, or to confirm it in them afterwards; and to desire such means as are impossible and not to be looked for, because they are contrary to the word of God. For the Apostle saith, At sundry times, and in divers manners God spake in the old time to our fathers by the Prophets; but in these last days he hath spoken unto us by his Son (Heb. c. 1. v. 1): that is, in the old time God did sundry ways declare his will unto men, as sometimes by visions when they were waking, and by dreams when they were sleeping, by Urim and Thummim in the Priest's breast, by Angels from heaven, by the Prophets, &c. but now he hath fully declared his will by his Son Christ, and hath appointed that we should come to the knowledge of it by that order which Christ

hath established ; who, when he ascended
up into heaven, gave unto his Church,
pastors and teachers, for the repairing of
the Saints, for the work of the ministry,
and for the edification of the body of
Christ, till we all meet together (in the
unity of faith, and the acknowledging of
the Son of God) unto a perfect man, and
unto the measure of the age of the fulness
of Christ (Eph. c. 4, v. 12) : therefore as
long as we live, we are to look for no other
means than these of pastors and teachers,
the other have ceased long ago, as being
appointed for the old world.

But yet unbelieving men refuse these,
and with itching ears they linger after the
other : and some are ready to say, Oh if I
might have an Angel come and tell me of
the destruction that shall come upon the
wicked for their sin, as Lot had in Sodom,
I would believe it (Gen. c. 19, v. 13): and
some are ready to say, if Lazarus might
come from the dead, that is, if some of
those my friends and acquaintance that are
dead, might rise out of their graves, and
come and tell me what they have seen and
felt in heaven and hell, if I might have but
a little conference with them, I would believe them. Or if I could see into the

heavens, and there behold Christ standing at the right hand of God, as Stephen the Martyr did (Acts c. 7, v. 56): or if I could hear him speak unto me from heaven, and call me from my sins, as Saul did, when he was a persecutor (c. 9, v. 4), then I would hearken unto him, and become a new man. And others think, Oh if they might be rapt into the third heavens, and be taken up into Paradise, as Paul was (2 Cor. c. 12, v. 4), and there hear God speak unto them, then they would perform great matters, and lead an Angel's life : or if being here on earth they might see God come down from heaven unto them, and they might have some sure token that it was he that spake unto them, as the Israel-ites had in the wilderness (Exod. c. 19, v. 20), when God spake there unto them upon Mount Sinai, then they would yield great obedience, and nothing should draw them from that which they had heard. These and many such foolish and impossi-ble things do men desire, and then they say they would believe all things, and until then they need not, neither will they.

But what saith the Apostle to the Ro-mans ? The righteousness which is of faith, speaketh on this wise, Say not in thine

heart, who shall ascend into heaven ? (that
is, to bring Christ from above :) or who shall
descend into the deep ? (that is, to bring
Christ from the dead.)   But what saith it ?
The word is near thee even in thy mouth,
and in thine heart ; this is the word of faith
which we preach (Rom. c. 10, v. 6).   Where
he sheweth what are the doubtful and wavering thoughts of unbelievers concerning
that salvation that is purchased for us by
Christ, and offered unto us in the Gospel ;
and how those thoughts and imaginations
by faith are to be repressed.   For they
which seek righteousness in themselves,
that by the works of the law they might be
justified and saved, being always unquiet
and doubtful of their salvation, because
they cannot find perfect righteousness in
themselves, are ready to say, if I might see
any Saint or Angel come from heaven to
carry me thither, or to assure me that I
shall come thither ; or any come from the
depth of hell to tell me that I am delivered
from thence, I could believe it.

But the righteousness of faith, that is,
true faith, whereby we are made righteous
in Christ, suppresseth these thoughts of
unbelief, and telleth us according to that
which is preached in the Gospel, that
Christ hath fulfilled all things needful for

our salvation, even that he hath suffered the curse of the law to deliver us from hell, and that he hath fulfilled the righteousness of the law to bring us to heaven, and he hath ascended up thither for us in our nature, to prepare a place for us: and he hath prayed unto God for us, that where he is we may be to behold his glory. Thus true faith for the certainty of our salvation, bids us rely upon that which Christ hath done for us, and upon that, which this way is set down in the Gospel; and so our consciences shall be quieted, and no man need to ask these questions who can ascend up into heaven, or bring us from hell? seeing that the Gospel teacheth that both these are done by Christ for all those that embrace their calling by a true faith.

But unbelief neglecting this, desireth that which is unreasonable, and saith, Oh, but I see none that hath ascended up to heaven, and come down again to tell me what is there done for me. Who shall ascend? who is he that hath, or will do so much? then I could believe it. And I see none that hath descended into hell, and returned to tell me that I am delivered from thence. Who shall descend into the deep? where is he that hath, or will do

this for me? then I could believe it. And
so not only the unbelievers are wholly possessed and overcome with these doubtful
thoughts; but all men, so far as unbelief
prevaileth in them, are ready to say thus,
at least in their hearts, Oh, if any might
come from heaven, to assure me that I
shall come thither, and be saved, then I
could believe it; or if any might come from
hell, to assure me that I am delivered from
thence, then I should be quiet in my mind,
and delivered from these fears that I am
encumbered with.

But what saith faith? Say not thus in
thine heart, &c. that is, have thou no such
doubts in thy mind, but consider what
Christ hath done for thee to bring thee to
heaven, and to deliver thee from hell; and
what the gospel doth this way offer unto
thee, and what thou hast heard preached
out of it to this end, and rest in them:
For if thou shalt confess with thy mouth
the Lord Jesus, and shalt believe in thine
heart that God raised him from the dead,
thou shalt be saved (Rom. c. 10, v. 9):
that is, if thou profess plainly and sincerely, and openly, that thou takest Jesus
only to be thy Lord and Saviour, and that
it was the very counsel and purpose of

God, in the resurrection of his son, to redeem us from death and hell, as it is
preached unto us in the Gospel, thou shalt
be saved. So faith leadeth us from these
vain speculations unto that which is revealed unto us in the word.

And whereas the best believers are subject unto these temptations at one time or
other, by reason of the remnants of unbelief abiding in them; yet the Apostle giveth
us to understand, that they come from unbelief, and not from faith; but that it is
in the nature of faith to strive against
them, and to suppress them in measure,
so far forth as faith prevaileth and getteth
the victory in them. So that when they
begin to have these doubts in their minds,
and to think with themselves how shall I
ascend into heaven? how shall I escape
hell? I cannot tell what shall become of
me! then faith is as a voice speaking behind them, to admonish them of their
duty, and, as it were pulling them by the
elbow, bids them hold their peace: Oh say
not in thine heart, who shall ascend into
heaven, &c. Oh have no such thoughts in
thy mind: this were to deny what Christ
hath done for thee concerning thy redemption from hell, and thy ascension into hea-

ven : therefore say not so in any case, no
not in thine heart : give over reasoning
with unbelief, and rest in the word of God.

Thus we see how unbelief bindeth God
to unreasonable courses, and desireth of
him for the strengthening of faith, things
not to be desired : therefore as we see from
whence such do arise, so we must strive
against unbelief, that we might overcome
such foolish conceits. And thus the unbelieving Jews did reason against our Saviour
Christ when he was upon the cross, and
thereby did shew what wicked and absurd
thoughts their infidelity did drive them
unto. If thou be the Son of God, come
down from the cross : he saved others, but
he cannot save himself (Matt. c. 27, v. 40) :
if he be the King of Israel, let him now
come down from the cross, and we will
believe in him (ver. 42) : he trusted in God,
let him deliver him now, if he will have
him : for he said, I am the Son of God
(ver. 43). Behold what unreasonable
things they do as it were bind Christ
unto, that they might believe in him, or
else they will not; for they say, let him
now come down from the cross, and now
save himself, or else never.

They did not consider how all the pro-

phesies of the Messiah set down in Scripture were verified in him, even from his
first conception unto this very hour ; how
he was conceived by the Holy Ghost, and
born of a virgin, and of the house of David,
and in Bethlehem ; how the wise men came
from the East unto Jerusalem, and told
them that the King of the Jews was born,
and that they had seen his star ; neither
what old father Simeon, and Anna the pro-
phetess said of him in the temple, when he
was circumcised. They regarded not his
doctrine full of authority and power, themselves being driven to confess, that never
man before spake like unto him : they
were not moved with his miracles, when
they saw how by his own power he healed
them of incurable diseases, made the blind
to see, the lame to go, the deaf to hear ;
cast out the devils by the power of his
word ; raised up them that were dead ; and
did many more things else, which were
sufficient to convince them that he was
the true Messiah and Saviour, to whom all
the Prophets gave witness ; neither did
they give any credit unto the voice of God
himself, which they heard from heaven,
when he was baptized, This is my beloved
Son, in whom I am well pleased (Mat. c. 3.

v. 17)': at what time also the heavens were opened, and the Spirit of God descended like a dove, and lighted upon him. Much less did they give credit unto the testimony of John, who said of him, Behold the Lamb of God, that taketh away the sins of the world (John c. 1, v. 36).

None of all these they regarded; they were not sufficient to cause them to believe in him, they despised them all, as though they had been nothing worth; but such a foolish thing as this they desire, and that should satisfy them — if he would come down from the cross, and that even very now' at their appointment, and tarry no longer than they could believe in him indeed; but if he would not do that at all, or not now presently without any delay, they will not believe in him. Which if he had done, he had forsaken his office of redemption, for he came to suffer and die for us, that he might, by his own sufferings, deliver us from death; and to die upon the cross, that he might redeem us from the curse of the law, being made a curse for us, as it is written, Cursed is every one that hangeth on a tree (Gal. c. 3, v. 13). And when he had suffered all things needful for our salvation, saying upon the cross, It is finished

(John c. 19, v. 30), and so gave up the
ghost, and afterwards was buried: God
raised him up at the time appointed, even
the third day, and loosed the sorrows of
death (Acts c. 2, v. 24), because it was impossible that he should be held of it any
longer, as St. Peter saith. But see the
foolishness of unbelief, the Jews would
have God then to deliver him before it was
time, even so soon as he was upon the
cross, and before he had suffered, or else
they would not believe that he was the Son
of God, or that he had any power to save
himself or others.

And after this manner the Devil teacheth
other men also by unbelief to reason against
good men, and against themselves; as if
such a man were an upright man, such an
one as he maketh shew of, God would not
suffer him to be so and so afflicted, but he
would deliver him from this cross that is
upon him: and so did the three friends of
Job reason against him to the great weakening of his faith: as this was also none of the
least temptations unto David, when the
wicked said of him in his misery, Where is
now thy God? (Psal. 42, v. 10): as if
they had said, Surely, if God were his
God, he would have delivered him long

before this. And of themselves they are
ready to say, if God would now deliver me
out of this affliction, if he would now help
me out of this trouble, I would think that
he had some care of me indeed ; and unless
they had some present ease or relief, they
cannot be persuaded of the truth of his promises. But what saith the Scripture?
Call upon me in the day of thy trouble;
so will I deliver thee (Psal. 50, v. 15). So
that we must seek unto God for the performance of his promises. But how? even
as it is said in another Psalm, Hear my
voice in the morning, O Lord : for in the
morning will I direct me unto thee, and I
will wait (Psal. 5, v. 3) : that is, after that
he had prayed unto God, he would patiently wait upon him with trust, till God
did shew that he had heard him. Even as
suitors do at the court, when they have
put up their petitions unto the King, or
the Council, though they have not a present answer, they are not discouraged, and
therefore give still attendance, and tarry
their leisure, with hope of speeding at the
last.

And how long must we thus wait upon
God for his deliverance? even until it
pleaseth him to discharge us; not pre-

scribing unto him any time. Even as it is said in one of the Psalms of degrees, My soul waiteth on the Lord, more than the morning watch watcheth for the morning (Psal. 130, v. 6): that is, even as they that are set to watch all night do not give over their station till the morning come, though the night be never so long: so we in affliction must not cease waiting upon God until the time appointed. And when is that? even when he giveth us our hearts desire, and not before. Even as the Psalmist speaketh in the name and person of the whole church, shewing after what manner, and how long he would seek unto God (Psal. 123, v. 2). Behold, as the eyes of servants look unto the hand of their masters, and as the eyes of a maid unto the hand of her mistress; so our eyes wait upon the Lord our God, until he have mercy upon us. So that he would continually and earnestly wait upon God for his defence, not doubting of it, until such time as he found it by experience; and therefore if he defer a while, we must tarry the longer, with good hope waiting. As the Prophet Habakkuk saith, that after long prayer he received this answer from the Lord concerning the deliverance of the

Church:—that it was deferred a long time, therefore he would have him to wait, for undoubtedly in time it should come, and not fail, saying, The vision is yet for an appointed time, but at the last it shall speak, and not lie: though it tarry, yet wait thou, for it shall surely come, and shall not stay (Habak. c. 2, v. 3).

But unbelief saith, I could believe these promises, if I might now enjoy them, and unless I be presently delivered, I cannot think that God regardeth me: and so it tieth God's favour to present deliverance. And though the Scripture hath said that affliction is like unto fire, and that our faith and patience is like unto gold; and therefore as the gold must tarry in the fire until all the dross be consumed, and the gold refined; so God will have us to endure the cross, until our corruption be thoroughly purged, and our faith and patience be proved to be pure and good; yet we are ready to say, that unless he deliver me now, I cannot believe that he hath any respect unto me. And unto all that which faith saith unto us, concerning the tarrying of God's leisure, unbelief is ready to make answer, that unless God give it now, I will think that I shall never have it. And as faith or unbelief prevaileth in us at any time, so are these thoughts more or less in us, in the time of any affliction: for the one is of the flesh, and the other of the Spirit, and both these being in the regenerate (Gal. c. 5, v. 17): The flesh lusteth against the Spirit, and the Spirit against the flesh; and these are contrary one to another: so that ye cannot do the same things that ye would, as Paul sheweth to the Galatians.

And this is that which every one of us hath experience of in ourselves; for how often when we have been in trouble, have we thought and said in our own hearts, unless God give me such and such means, there are none that will do me good; and unless these help me, I cannot look for help from any: and so we are ready to tie God's help to times and to means. Whereas faith saith otherwise out of the word of God, namely, that he hath other times and means in his hands to do us good by, and that he is able to help us when all means fail us. And besides, what if he will not deliver us at all? but will have us drink of that cup which he hath given us, even unto death; as Christ himself did: his love is never a whit the less unto us no more than it was unto him. Thus we see, how

this unbelief reigneth in this world, and
yet how Christ, of his infinite goodness and
mercy, beareth with those that are his in it
for a while, and cureth them of it at the
last, as he did with the Apostle Thomas,
and as he hath done with us very often, and
in many things.

And this is that which the Prophet
noteth to have been very often in the people of Israel, whilst they were in the wilderness, of whom he saith, They returned,
and tempted God, and limited the holy one
of Israel (Psal. 78, v. 41): that is, according to the straitness of their own heart
in their unbelief, so did they imagine of
God's presence and power; and therefore
they are said to limit the holy one of
Israel, and as it were to compass him in
certain bounds, and to indent with him
after this manner:—if he would do so and
so for them, they would think that he cared
for them, and were among them for their
good; and if he would not do so, they would
not believe it. And thus they did often,
and therefore it is said, they returned and
tempted God; for when they had tempted
God thus one way, then they did it
another way. For sometimes they desired
water, sometimes meat, sometimes dainty

flesh, as quails; and that so importunately, that they said unless they had these things according to their own desire, they thought either that God could not do it, or that he cared not for them: and thus they spake against God, saying, Can God prepare a table in the wilderness? behold, he smote the rock that the waters gushed out, and the streams overflowed: can he give bread also, and prepare flesh for his people? (ver. 19). And thus did not only once, but many times, and for many things; insomuch that the Prophet speaketh with admiration, How oft did they provoke him in the wilderness, and grieve him in the desert! (ver. 40). And thus for their assurance that God was with them, and that he was willing and able to help them, they desired these outward things, and so by the foolishness of their desires did apparently shew the unbelief that was in them.

So do many unbelievers of our time: look what they earnestly desire, if they have it not, they will not believe that God careth for them: and hereupon some of them say, if I might have such a thing, I would think that God loved me: and others says, if God would bestow this or that upon me, I would hope that I were in his favour. And what things are they then which they desire? only outward, and appertaining to this life: and so according to their present wants through unbelief they limit the love of God, some to one thing, some to another, and will not be persuaded of it, but by the enjoying of such things as themselves desire.

And it is thus not only in the unbelievers; but all God's children, so far as the remnants of unbelief do prevail in them, are subject unto these temptations, and to these desires; and are ready to say, if I were rid of this affliction which hath lien heavily upon me a long time, I could be persuaded of his favour towards me. By which we are thus to profit, thereby to see what infidelity is lurking in us, that so we might be sorry for it, and seek to be holpen of it. And then we shall see the remedy against it to be this:—that as the Apostle St. Thomas should not have tied the certainty of Christ's resurrection, to his apparition and shewing of himself unto him, saying, Unless I see him myself, I will not believe it: for it was true, and to be believed of him and others, that Christ was risen again, though they had never seen him; much less should he have tied

it unto this, that he would see him in that
form that he was in upon the cross, with
the wounds and marks in his body, saying,
Unless I see in his hands the print of the
nails, and put my finger into the print of
the nails, and put my hand into his side, I
will not believe it ; for he might have appeared unto him in some other form, as he
did unto others, at divers times.

Even so we are not to tie the certainty of
God's favour to any one thing, and to say,
unless I have this or that, I cannot be persuaded of God's favour : much less unto
any of these outward things, which apper-
tain unto our bodies and to this life ; for
God our heavenly Father hath many ways
and means to assure his children of his
love and favour towards them ; and doth it
as our earthly fathers do, not only to some
one way, and to others another way, but
even unto the same not alike at all times,
and by the same things. But especially
there are more sure pledges and tokens of
his love, which he bestoweth upon his
children, than all the outward benefits in
the world ; which only for the most part
the unbelievers desire, and measure God's
favour by them. For there are the graces
and gifts of his holy Spirit proper unto the

elect, as a love of God and of goodness, an
hatred of evil, a desire to please God, a
delight in the company of the godly, and
such like: in bestowing of which upon
man, he doth most of all manifest his love
unto them. There are also his holy word
and sacraments, whereby he worketh the
beginning and increase of these and other
graces in those that are his : rare and ines-
timable testimonies of his favour! of which
it is said in the Psalm (147, v. 19), He
sheweth his word unto Jacob, his statutes
and his judgments unto Israel: he hath
not dealt so with every nation, neither
have they known his judgments. Where
he maketh this a note of the love of God to
the people of the Jews, above all other nations, that they had among them the doctrine of everlasting life, which others wanted.
And so this is none of the least testimonies
of God's favour towards us, that we live in
these happy days and blessed times, in
which the Gospel is purely and sincerely
preached, and that we enjoy the ministry
of it.

But the greatest token of all, whereby
God hath manifested his love unto us, is
the death of his Son ; of which Christ
speaketh in the Gospel, God so loved the

world, that he gave his only begotten Son, that whosoever believeth in him should not perish, but have everlasting life (John c. 1, v. 10): where he noteth the excellency of the love of God, by the excellency of the gift. He so loved the world with an extraordinary and wonderful great love, that he gave his only begotten Son to save us: and this is the fountain and cause of all other benefits of his bestowed, and to be bestowed upon us; as the Apostle saith (Rom. c. 8, v. 32), God that spared not his own Son, but gave him for us all to death, how shall he not with him give us all things also? and by him there are purchased and prepared for us everlasting joys in the kingdom of heaven: and though we want many things in this world, yet God giveth us patience, and minds well contented with our estate, as a token that he loveth us. So that by all these things, or by any one of them, and by many more, is God's love known and to be believed. Therefore we must not be so foolish to stint God by unbelief, and say, if I may have this or that I will be persuaded of his favour; for there are other things besides those which we imagine, whereby he may manifest his favour unto us most clearly;

and that also not only in this world, but in the world to come: not only which we have in present possession, but which we enjoy through hope.

And therefore this is singularly commended in the faith of Job, that when he had lost all his worldly goods, and in respect of his outward estate, he was brought unto nothing; yet he did put his trust in God; believing that his favour was not tied to them, nor to any one of them; but that it was the same then, that it was before; and so uttered this comfortable speech, proceeding from faith in God's goodness:—Naked came I out of my mother's womb, and naked shall I return thither: the Lord hath given, and the Lord hath taken it, blessed be the name of the Lord (Job c. 1, v. 21). He doth not say, if God would restore all unto me again (as he did in time, yea he doubled them) then I would believe that he cared for me: but even while he remained in the want of all, he blessed and praised the name of God; which could not be without great faith. Yea he said further, that if he should die in that estate, yet he would put his trust in God, and believe that he cared for him:—Lo! though he slay me, yet will I trust in

him, and he shall be my salvation (Job
c. 13, v. 15): in which words he confesseth, that he was so far, even in this great
extremity, from despairing of life or salvation, as that in the very power and instant
of death he would trust in him; for he had
other testimonies of God's favour than all
his outward prosperity; even the testimony
of a good conscience, that he had walked
before him in sincerity and truth, and that
he had been no hypocrite; as he declareth
at large in chap. 31.

And he had further, for the upholding
of his faith, the constant truth of God's
promises; and those not only for this life,
but for the life to come; and therefore he
doubted not, but that it should go well
with him, though he died in that estate;
for he hoped at the last day to rise again,
and to behold Christ his Saviour to his
everlasting comfort; when he saith, Oh
that my words were now written, oh that
they were written even in a book (Job c. 19,
v. 23): and graven with an iron pen, in
lead or in stone for ever; for I am sure
that my redeemer liveth, and he shall
stand the last on the earth: and though
after my skin worms destroy this body, yet
shall I see God in my flesh, whom I shall

see myself, and my eyes shall behold, and none other for me, though my reins are consumed within me. Where we see how he saith, that in the midst of all his afflictions he did rejoice and glory in this, even in the testimony of a good conscience, whereby he did so rest in the promises of God concerning his resurrection and life eternal, which was to come, that this did confirm him in the favour of God against all temptations.

Thus true faith bindeth not God's favour to any of these outward things, whereby men do commonly desire to be assured of it; but it looketh unto better things, whereby his love is most apparent; and that not only in this life, but in the life to come most of all; as they be promised and set down in the word of God. And that is the remedy against the foolish and vain desires of unbelief. Let us not, therefore, tie the assurance of God's favour unto any one thing, but seeing that he hath many ways to declare it, let us believe the promises of his word, and pray him to seal them up in our hearts by what means it shall please him best: and let us not be so froward and perverse, as to think it is not constant unto us, unless it be sealed up that way which we ourselves do most of all desire.

Therefore to conclude the sum of all in few words, we see by the weakness of St. Thomas, not only what we are subject unto, but also how we may help ourselves and others against the same. He did not believe that Christ was risen again, though it was told him at sundry times by divers, that were very credible: we must therefore in the matter of faith give credit unto the word of God brought unto us, in the mouths of his faithful servants, if they be but two or three. Secondly, he in this case would believe none but himself: we must believe in the mystery of our salvation others rather than ourselves, and think, especially that in the time of temptation, others are able better to judge of our estate than we ourselves can, and so be not too much addicted to our own overweaning.

Thirdly, he would believe nothing of this matter any further than himself was able to see and feel: now because these may deceive us, we must believe without any sight or feeling; especially seeing that faith is of things that are not seen, and the favour of God is not always sensible of his benefits, we must believe his word without;

yea contrary to any thing that we can see or feel. Lastly, he would not believe except he saw Christ with his wounds, and so in that form which, ordinarily, was not to be looked for: we therefore must not by unbelief tie the testimonies of God's favour for the assurance of our faith unto such things as are unreasonable, and commonly not to be looked for; neither unto any one particular thing, because he hath many ways to confirm the same unto us; and pray him to give us grace, that we may profit in faith by any that he shall bestow upon us.

And seeing it is so hard a thing to believe, and there is so much infidelity hidden in the hearts of the best servants of God; let us labour to search into the depth of our own, that finding the same in ourselves, we may, while we have time, use in fear all those good means that God hath appointed for the beginning and increase of faith in us, that so by his blessing, we daily going on forward from faith to faith, we may at the last come to that measure of it, against which the very gates of hell be not able to prevail; that so we may, both in temptation and under all crosses, and in the hour of death, so carry ourselves as God may be glorified, we ourselves may be comforted, and others may be furthered by our Christian calling and good example: which Christ, the author and finisher of our faith, grant unto us, for his own name sake: to whom, with the Father and the Holy Spirit, one true, immortal, invisible, and only wise God, be ascribed as most due, all honour, praise, and glory for ever and ever. Amen.

Nichols, Son, and Bentley, Printers,
Red Lion Passage, Fleet Street, London.

Ingram Content Group UK Ltd.
Milton Keynes UK
UKHW022007030523
421159UK00006B/230

9 781375 453295